VALENCIA

TOP EXPERIENCES · LOCAL LIFE

ANDY SYMINGTON

Contents

Plan Your Trip 4

La Catedral (p50)
MISTERVLAD/SHUTTERSTOCK ©

Explore
Valencia   33

Worth a Trip

Special Features

Survival
Guide   147

COVID-19

We have re-checked every business in this book before publication to ensure that it is still open after the COVID-19 outbreak. However, the economic and social impacts of COVID-19 will continue to be felt long after the outbreak has been contained, and many businesses, services and events referenced in this guide may experience ongoing restrictions. Some businesses may be temporarily closed, have changed their opening hours and services, or require bookings; some unfortunately could have closed permanently. We suggest you check with venues before visiting for the latest information.

Valencia's
Top Experiences

Attend a Concert in the Ciudad de las Artes y las Ciencias (p80)

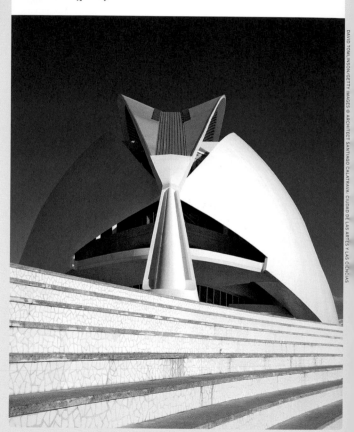

DAVID TOMLINSON/GETTY IMAGES © ARCHITECT SANTIAGO CALATRAVA, CIUDAD DE LAS ARTES Y LAS CIENCIAS

Find the Holy Grail at La Catedral (p50)

Check Out the Door of Sin at La Lonja (p56)

See Art in a Former Seminary at Museo de Bellas Artes (p108)

Wander the Renaissance Courtyard of Museo del Patriarca (p36)

NEIL FARRIN/GETTY IMAGES ©

MASSIMO TODARO/SHUTTERSTOCK ©

Sip Wine and Watch the Bustle in Mercado Central (p54)

Wander the Wetlands of La Albufera (p140)

See the Views from Hilltop Castillo de Sagunto (p142)

FERNANDO.RM/SHUTTERSTOCK ©

INU/SHUTTERSTOCK ©

Uncover Layers of History at Xàtiva (p144)

Dining Out

Valencia has a fabulous eating culture combining quality local ingredients, pan-Mediterranean influences and modern Spanish techniques. Whether you're trying avant-garde tapas or a traditional pan of rice, eating out is a major highlight. As is common in Spain, most restaurants don't open until 8pm, and even later on weekends.

Rice

Valencia's most famous speciality is its rice dishes, which include but are not limited to paellas. There's an incredible variety; you'll find them bursting with ingredients from turnips to snails to lobster. Locals are very particular about them, and will judge the quality of the *socarrat* – the crust on the bottom – like a vintage wine.

Tapas

Valencia has a thriving tapas culture, and the quality of these dishes is astonishingly high. Unlike in other parts of Spain, locals tend to sit down and order tapas dishes at tables, so many 'tapas bars' have more of a restaurant feel than a bar ambience.

The Huerta

Valencia is surrounded by its *huerta,* a fertile agricultural floodplain filled with market gardens irrigated by a series of channels devised by the Moors. A source of great pride to Valencians, the *huerta* supplies the city with delightfully fresh produce, especially vegetables, citrus fruit and rice.

Where to Eat

The main eating zones are the Barrio del Carmen, L'Eixample and, above all, the vibrant tapas-packed streets of Russafa.

Best Dining

El Poblet Quique Dacosta's Valencian place offers top-notch gastronomy. (p41)

Ricard Camarena Stunning modern cuisine from the city's foremost chef. (p115)

Dos Estaciones Two-chef team produces wonders from an open kitchen. (p99)

Refugio Very pleasing fusion cuisine at sharp prices. (p73)

Gran Azul Fabulous seafood and steaks in this spacious and elegant grill. (p115)

NADIESHDA/GETTY IMAGES ©

Navarro Brilliant spot for rice, which has been going for generations. (p41)

Entrevins Elegant upstairs retreat with a focus on fine food and wine. (p62)

El Pederniz Worth seeking out for top game and meat dishes. (p134)

Balansiya Excellent North African cooking in a beautiful, soothing setting. (p115)

Best Tapas

Bodega Casa Montaña Ultracharactertul old bodega with sensational seafood tapas. (p123)

Canalla Bistro Playful fusion tapas from a famous chef. (p100)

Delicat A cordial couple drum up some very tasty tapas medleys. (p63)

Bar Ricardo Valencian classic with professional service and glorious food. (p134)

Bar Cabanyal Youthful venue for excellent seafood flavours. (p125)

El Tap Good value for original, market-based tapas in the Carmen. (p73)

El Rodamón de Russafa A tapas journey around the globe. (p97)

Tanto Monta Legendary in the student zone for its little open sandwiches. (p116)

Tasca Ángel No-frills joint known for its grilled sardines – delicious. (p63)

L'Ostrería del Carme Simple market stall doing cracking oysters and white wine. (p75)

Best Vegetarian & Vegan

Casa Viva Cheery Russafa locale for creative veggie and vegan fare. (p100)

Copenhagen Bright and cheerful in central Russafa. (p101)

La Lluna Old school backstreet vegetarian that's still going strong. (p76)

La Tastaolletes Creative veggie tapas and larger meals in a breezy modern environment. (p75)

Cinnamon A tiny space that nevertheless produces some deliciously creative fare, with good vegetarian options. (p63)

Las Lunas Great lunch menu with a daily vegan choice. (p88)

Bar Open

Valencia has vibrant, multifaceted nightlife. The Barrio del Carmen comes to life at the weekend, Russafa has a great vibe, and students pump the Northeast. Much nightlife relocates to the beach and marina in summer, with a range of discotecas (clubs) and some year-round offbeat gems here too.

Barrio del Carmen

The *barrio* (neighbourhood) is quiet midweek, but its shutters come up on weekend evenings, revealing a starburst of little bars. Decent cafes are easy to find at any time.

Russafa

Russafa has the best bar scene, with a huge range of everything from family-friendly cultural cafes to quirky bars, and a couple of big clubs. In the main, though, it's a place for some quiet evening beers or after-dinner drinks rather than rampant all-nighters.

The Northeast

The university area, especially around Avenidas de Aragón and Blasco Ibáñez, has enough bars and *discotecas* to keep you busy all night. Thursday is traditionally the night students head out to get hammered, but this is also the city's main nightclub area at weekends. Benimaclet has some lovely alternative options.

Best Bars & Cafes

Café Negrito Socially aware cafe-bar on a tucked-away square. (p65)

Jimmy Glass Dimly lit spot with a great jazz soundtrack. (p76)

La Fábrica de Hielo A bit of everything at this intriguing spot near the sea. (p128)

Tyris on Tap Excellent microbrewed beer in a trendily industrial setting. (p65)

Ubik Café Very cosy cafe, bar and bookshop that makes a comfy spot to lurk. (p102)

Sant Jaume Pocket-sized bar with a great people-watching terrace. (pictured; p66)

ANDREA PISTOLESI/GETTY IMAGES ©

Beat Brew Bar One of the city's most serious spots for coffee. (p67)

Café Museu A landmark bohemian local in the heart of the Barrio del Carmen. (p76)

Kaf Café Exemplar of the alternative cultural vibe of Benimaclet. (p117)

Cuatro Monos Popular spot in Russafa for craft beer and Italian snacks. (p103)

L'Ermità Laneway bar with a cosy interior and good music. (p76)

Mercado de Colón Sip a little something in the open-plan elegance of this Modernista jewel. (p91)

Café de las Horas An extravagant baroque interior makes this a characterful venue for a drink. (p66)

Slaughterhouse This former butchery is now a place to meet, not a place for meat. (p102)

La Casa de la Mar Sip on a cold one as you inhale the surfer vibe. (p128)

Café Bla Bla The elegant straight man in the student nightlife zone. (p118)

La Batisfera This family-friendly place is both a bookshop and bar. (p128)

Best Clubs

L'Umbracle Terraza/Mya Alfresco drinking in an amazing setting plus a club downstairs. (p91)

Radio City A variety of events, and DJs or live music every night. (p67)

Marina Beach Club Phenomenally popular bar and club right on the water. (p128)

Akuarela Playa One of the main coastal nightclubs driving the pumping summer scene. (p129)

Piccadilly Downtown Club Appealing Russafa option for some dance-floor action. (p97)

Deseo 54 A mixed young crowd at this popular *discoteca*. (p117)

Rumbo 144 Late-opening student favourite in the university district. (p118)

Treasure Hunt

As you might expect from a big city, Valencia has a wealth of shopping opportunities. All of Spain's big-name clothing stores are present, but there's also a thriving scene for smaller-scale, locally designed clothing and accessories. Unique pieces, like a Lladró porcelain or a hand-painted fan, can make special souvenirs.

Shopping Central

The southern part of the old city is Valencia's main commercial area, with a major department store surrounded by streets packed with options. This zone melds into L'Eixample, where the area around the Mercado de Colón is replete with high-end boutiques, delis and other intriguing shops.

Offbeat Shopping

On the fringes of these areas, you'll find quirkier, offbeat shopping experiences, such as Russafa, full of hipster clothing stores and vintage shops. Within the old centre, the Barrio del Carmen and the streets near the Mercado Central have fascinating smaller shops.

Best Food & Drink

Mercado Central Fabulous downtown venue for fresh produce. (p54)

Mercat Municipal del Cabanyal Traditional covered market with high-quality comestibles. (p123)

Bodegas Baviera Glorious wine shop with bags of character. (p67)

Mercado de Mossén Sorell Sweet little market for gourmet bites. (p77)

Trufas Martínez Historic chocolate truffles. (p93)

Manglano Excellent deli produce and wine in the Mercado de Colón. (p93)

Turrones Ramos Get your essential Spanish Christmas nougat here. (p44)

Best Alternative & Vintage

Madame Mim Excellent destination for vintage clothing and unusual items. (p104)

Pannonica Quirky shop for vintage clothes and other items. (p77)

Santo Spirito Vintage Spacious destination for classic American and British styles. (p77)

TUPUNGATO/SHUTTERSTOCK ©

Lakajade Vintage Where the folk of Benimaclet go for retro rags. (p119)

Place A creative space with multiple stallholders. (p93)

Paranoid Design your own T-shirt or pick up a weird electronic instrument. (p105)

Vinyl Eye Lovably unusual shop with rock-inspired prints for T-shirts. (p137)

Best Boutiques & Clothing

Sombreros Albero Pick up a trilby from these traditional hat-makers. (p43)

Linda Vuela A Rio Top-drawer perfumery sourcing exquisite global scents. (p92)

Lladró Famous local porcelain sculptures. (p45)

Madame Bugalú Stylish, sassy women's clothing. (p67)

Pángala Handmade bags with plenty of non-animal products. (p77)

100% Pirata Breezy, stylish, eclectic clothes for women. (p137)

Best Gifts & Souvenirs

Abanicos Carbonell Valencian fans for Valencia fans. (p92)

Kowalski Bellas Artes Unusual and enchanting art shop. (p104)

Al Vent Pleasing little stop for good-value handmade jewellery. (p77)

Valencia Club de Fútbol Megastore Shirts, scarves and more from the top local football side. (p45)

Cestería El Globo Basketwork, wooden toys and other surprises. (p43)

Plaza Redonda Several handicrafts stores around one central 'square'. (p45)

Artesanía Yuste Enchanting hand-painted ceramics in the centre. (p67)

Galería 4 Exhibitions of captivating, affordable contemporary art. (p44)

Museums & Galleries

Befitting a city of its size, Valencia has a wealth of museums covering its history, industries, festivals and other aspects of life. Several galleries offer an excellent overview of Spanish art across the centuries. Most of these places, many of which are housed in intriguing buildings, are within an easy walk of the centre of town.

Temporary Exhibitions

One of Valencia's real fortes is the number of spaces that attract excellent temporary exhibitions. While it's not quite Barcelona or Madrid, there's always something worthwhile on, so it pays to check with the tourist office or online to see what's on, where.

Municipal Museums

Valencia has some two dozen municipal museums, all of which cost €2 and are free on Sunday. For a €6 combined ticket, you can get entry to all of them for three days. There are numerous other combined entry tickets – get the tourist office to run through the options with you.

Best Museums

Museo de las Ciencias Príncipe Felipe This notable modern building houses a super interactive science museum. (p81)

Museo Nacional de Cerámica In a flamboyant palace, this excellent museum covers the important Valencian ceramics industry. (p39)

L'Almoina Descend under the old town to see layers of history unfolded before your eyes. (p61)

Museo de Etnología This visual, conceptual exhibition of ethnology is very easy on the eye and lots of fun. (p71)

Museo de Historia de Valencia See how Valencia changed through the ages in this romantic brick-vaulted water deposit. (p133)

Museo de la Seda Explore the history of Valencia's famous silk industry. (p39)

Museo de Arroz This former rice mill shows you the machinery that produced Valencia's favourite grain. (p123)

Museo Fallero A charming rogue's gallery of the favourite sculpture characters from each year of the Fallas festival. (p87)

ELEPHOTOS/SHUTTERSTOCK ©

Town Hall Within this impressive civic building is a museum on the city's history. (p40)

L'Iber An astonishing collection of toy soldiers makes this a very out-of-the-ordinary visit. (p72)

Best Galleries & Exhibition Spaces

Museo de Bellas Artes Valencia's excellent main art gallery has a strong selection of Spanish paintings. (pictured; p108)

Museo del Patriarca Small but superb, this seminary's collection of 16th-century art is remarkable. (p36)

Institut Valencià d'Art Modern A major contemporary art gallery with a small but impressive permanent collection plus touring exhibitions. (p71)

Museo Catedralicio Diocesano Fine selection of art in the museum within the cathedral itself. (p53)

Almudín A huge 15th-century city granary that houses exhibitions but is worth a visit for the building alone. (p61)

Centro Cultural Bancaja This bank's cultural foundation brings in excellent art exhibitions with free entry a bonus. (p61)

Bombas Gens Attractive conversion of a former pump factory into an exhibition space. (p113)

Centro del Carmen This former monastery cloister is an attractive space for temporary exhibitions. (p72)

Centro Cultural La Nau The old university building in the centre of town has regular and interesting exhibitions. (p40)

Luis Adelantado Stylish, carefully curated contemporary art exhibitions are held in this central gallery. (p40)

Reales Atarazanas These Gothic shipyard warehouses near the port make an intriguing venue for temporary exhibitions. (p123)

Sporting Club Russafa Drop by to see what's on in this cooperative artists' collective. (p99)

Las Naves Buzzing arts centre near the port with regular exhibitions. (p125)

Architecture

The rich architectural legacy that is so characteristic of Mediterranean cities is very much the story in Valencia. Periods of occupation and influence combined with flourishing overseas trade to create a dynamic city prone to innovation, from Roman urbanism to Calatrava's caprices via Moorish elegance, Gothic majesty and Modernista swirls.

Modernisme

The local form of the art nouveau or Jugendstil revolution in architecture and design had Barcelona as its base, but was hugely influential here in Valencia too. Modernisme added whimsical motifs, often based on nature, to buildings and sought to play with rigid neoclassical ideas of straight lines. Wealthy merchants patronised promising architects and built grand houses in the new expansion districts outside the city walls. L'Eixample in Valencia is a treasure trove of such buildings, as you'll see on our themed walking tour (p59).

Calatrava

One of the world's most famous living architects, local boy Santiago Calatrava first achieved renown with his fluid, striking bridges. Their often skeletal design themes were later incorporated into ambitious building projects the world over. His buildings at the Ciudad de las Artes y Ciencias in his hometown are, despite the budgeting and other problems, extraordinary by any measure.

Best Gothic, Moorish & More

La Lonja One of the great Gothic civil buildings left to us, with a stunning main hall. (pictured; p56)

Torres de Quart This magnificent gateway, one of only two structures remaining from the city wall, gateway is a striking sight. (p71)

Torres de Serranos Like its sibling Quart, this imposing gateway is a glorious monument. (p71)

Catedral The mostly Gothic cathedral dominates the centre of town. (p50)

Centro del Carmen This exhibition space occupies a

ELROCE/SHUTTERSTOCK ©

handsome Gothic cloister. (p72)

Almudín The scale and design of this medieval city granary are extraordinary. (p61)

Castillo de Xàtiva This eagle's-nest fortress offers sturdy military architecture from a variety of periods. (p144)

Palau de la Generalitat A handsome Gothic palace is the seat of regional government. (p62)

Reales Atarazanas Though much changed over the years, these Gothic warehouses are still an impressive sight. (p123)

Baños del Almirante The structure of this typical Moorish bathhouse has been well conserved. (p62)

Castillo de Sagunto The imposing wall of this sizeable castle compound stretches between two hilltops. (p142)

Best Baroque, Modernista & Modern

Ciudad de las Artes y las Ciencias Calatrava's controversial collection of buildings were expensive but are a stunning testament to his creativity. (p80)

Palacio del Marqués de Dos Aguas Extravagant doesn't even begin to do justice to this outrageously flamboyant rococo mansion. (p39)

Estación del Norte This train station is a heartwarming Modernista gem, with numerous optimismfilled details. (p39)

Mercado de Colón This stunning Modernista market building is one of the city's highlights of the style. (p87)

Museo de Historia de Valencia The intriguing crypt like space was a 19th-century water deposit. (p133)

Town Hall This handsome neoclassical building dominates the Plaza del Ayuntamiento. (p40)

Mercado Central The vast Modernista central market is still the city's main hub of fresh produce. (p54)

Institut Valencià d'Art Modern Impressively designed contemporary art gallery. (p71)

Espai Vert This 1980s architectural project aimed at rethinking communal living is an astonishing sight. (p111)

Kids

Valencia is an easy place to take kids. Hotels are used to requests for extra beds and often have connecting rooms or family suites. The plethora of apartment rental options is also handy. The beaches are a good attraction, and riding there in the speedy tram is fun too. The other great playground is the diverted Turia's former 9km riverbed.

PAOLO CERTO/SHUTTERSTOCK ©

Bioparc This innovative zoo recreates African landscapes and gets you up close to the animals. (p133)

Oceanogràfic This massive aquarium, divided into climate zones, could keep the family spellbound for hours. (pictured; p87)

Museo de las Ciencias Príncipe Felipe This hands-on science museum is fabulous for kids aged 12 and over. (p81)

Hemisfèric With a planetarium, IMAX cinema and laser show, this is high-approval family entertainment. (p81)

Jardines del Turia Some 9km of traffic-free park with numerous playgrounds and playmates. (p113)

Gulliver Unleash the little ones to climb up and slide down this ever-patient recumbent giant. (p139)

Playa de las Arenas This is the easiest-reached of the beaches, with a lively family scene. (p125)

Valencia Club de Fútbol Take the kids to see one of Spain's biggest football teams. (p118)

Teatro la Estrella Enchanting puppet shows are put

on at weekends in this cute theatre. (p137)

Valencia Basket Club Little visited by non-locals, the Spanish basketball league is a family-friendly evening out. (p93)

Mercado de Colón Kick back on a terrace while the kids play safely in this handsome market building. (p91)

L'Iber A whole world of toy soldiers. (p72)

Family Savings

The various attractions at the **Ciudad de las Artes y las Ciencias** (p80) are fun but far from free, so do research the range of family and combined tickets available online.

Live Music & Theatre

With a vibrant theatre scene and two architecturally and acoustically excellent concert halls, Valencia is a hub for performing arts. The live-music culture in smaller venues is active too, covering flamenco to boogaloo to garage. Various magazines available at tourist offices and newspaper kiosks are handy for checking upcoming events.

CHRISTIAN BERTRAND/SHUTTERSTOCK ©

Palau de les Arts Reina Sofía This stupendous Calatrava building hosts mostly opera, but also classical concerts. (p92)

Radio City Something different on every night in this cultural icon of a bar. (p67)

Black Note Popular and well-established venue for live jazz, funk, soul and more. (p118)

Jimmy Glass Regular live jazz in this atmospheric central venue. (p76)

Wah Wah The favourite alternative music venue for many, Wah Wah is a legend in its own right. (pictured; p118)

Espacio Inestable Tucked away in the northeast of the old town, this edgy space has great movement and dance performances. (p67)

Teatro Principal As you might guess from the name, this is one of Valencia's main theatres. (p43)

Loco Club There's a solid programme of live music from local and touring acts at this reliable venue. (p137)

Café del Duende Valencia's best venue for flamenco, this is a small, intimate spot. (p137)

Palau de la Música Right on the 'river', this has a good program of mostly classical music recitals. (p139)

16 Toneladas By the bus station, this venue has regular live rock bands and is also a nightclub. (p119)

Matisse Club Live music almost nightly, from classical to rock. (p119)

Café Mercedes Jazz Russafa jazz venue with top-notch sound. (p104)

Teatro la Estrella Weekend puppet shows aimed at families. (p137)

Teatre El Musical In the fishing *barrio* of El Cabanyal, this venue has regular concerts alongside its program of community theatre. (p129)

Parks & Outdoor Spaces

INU/SHUTTERSTOCK ©

Jardines del Turia The former riverbed is now a standout strip of park that gives the whole city a green artery. (p113)

Ciudad de las Artes y las Ciencias The visual impact as you walk around the precinct stays long in the memory. (p80)

Bioparc An innovative zoo that presents the animals in beautifully landscaped 'African' surroundings. (p133)

La Albufera Gorgeous lagoonscapes, beaches, birdwatching and rice paddies. (p140)

Plaza de la Virgen The spiritual heart of the old town, centred on a fountain representing the Turia. (pictured; p61)

Puente de las Flores A riot of flowers covers a bridge across the Turia. (p139)

Jardín Botánico This university-run walled garden is a welcome retreat from the powerful sun. (p133)

Jardines del Real A lovely spot for a stroll, with plenty of palms and oranges in what were once the grounds of a palace. (p113)

Parque Central Romantic, newly opened formal park in former rail yards. (p99)

Convent Carmen Grab a beer and some street food and relax in this former cloister. (p72)

Playa de las Arenas, **Playa de la Malvarrosa** and **Playa de la Patacona** These three city beaches are really one long strip of sand, great for strolling. (p125)

L'Umbracle Terraza Sip a cocktail under the stars at this stylish summer venue. (p91)

Jardín de las Hespérides A formal garden in French style just on the edge of the old town. (p133)

Sant Jaume Our favourite spot to sip a drink on a central terrace and watch life go by. (p66)

Akuarela Playa This *discoteca* has a huge outdoor area for summer clubbing by the sea. (p129)

Parque de Cabecera This landscaped park has lakes, a hill with vistas and ample strolling space. (p139)

LGBTIQ+

NEDROFLY/SHUTTERSTOCK ©

Valencia is a very gay-friendly place, with an extremely relaxed attitude to sexuality. In some ways, that means that there's far less of a separate scene here, with a mix of folk to be expected in any bar or restaurant in Russafa or the Barrio del Carmen, for example. Nevertheless, there are some thriving LGBTIQ+ bars and clubs.

Russafa

Russafa is a bustling post-scene locale and a testament to the open-minded attitude of Valencia. Friendliness is a given around here and the distinction between LGBTIQ+-friendly and hetero-friendly is so blurred as to usually not exist. This is a fine place to meet people in relaxed pre-club surroundings.

Beaches

Of the city beaches, the northern part of Playa de la Malvarrosa (pictured) is the most popular. South of Valencia, in La Albufera region, Playa de l'Arbre del Gos is the region's main gay beach and is spacious, attractive and frequented by men and women. It's clothing optional. To find it, head north from El Saler beach or south from Pinedo. Look for a disused chimney stack. Buses 14 and 15 reach Pinedo, while 25 hits El Saler.

Best LGBTIQ+ Bars

Trapezzio The LGBTIQ+ crowd in the Barrio del Carmen is well established and an important part of the local community. This is a fixture. (p76)

Deseo 54 Young and beautiful people predominate in this nightclub; it's a mixed crowd. (p117)

Planet Valencia A kicking Russafa bar that's lots of fun for lesbians. (p102)

La Boba y el Gato Rancio Casual and relaxed LGBTIQ+-friendly bar and cafe in Russafa. (p102)

Pub Bubu Bears and their friends will find their den here. (p137)

Under The Radar

The bulk of Valencia's visitors concentrate on the big-ticket sites in the Ciutat Vella, with a trip to the Ciudad de las Artes y Ciencias added on. But there is an intriguing range of attractions, from quirky museums to well-loved local tapas haunts, beyond those areas.

GREG ELMS/LONELY PLANET ©

Local Barrios

To get under the skin of Valencia and really experience the city, you can't do better than getting a feel for barrio life. While this can still be found in pockets in the Ciutat Vella, it pays to go beyond it to the districts where most Valencians live. Here you will find local cafes and bars, fabulous places to eat and quirky cultural hubs.

Good areas to begin your exploration are the north-ern and eastern suburbs (including Benimaclet, see p), the southern stretches of L'Eixample and the west of the city. It's also great to push further out by bike, car or public transport, and explore some of the villages beyond the city limits, where Valencia's huerta (region of market gardens) supplies fabulous fresh produce to the province.

Best Under the Radar Valencia

Bombas Gens Former factory converted into intriguing modern arts space. (p113)

Horta Viva Tours and events in the market garden villages that surround the city. (p25)

Museo de Historia de Valencia Off-the-beaten-track museum of city history (pictured: p133).

Bar Rausell Locals in the know flock here at lunchtime. (p134)

Valencia Basket Club Head on down to catch a league game. (p93)

Museo de Arroz Restored mill that gives the history of rice production in the region. (p123)

La Fábrica de Hielo Always something intriguing going on at this former ice factory near the beach. (p128)

Las Naves Former warehouse that is now a humming creative hub. (p125)

Balansiya Authentic and delicious Moroccan food in a local barrio. (p115)

La Murta Coffee and tapas stop in the heart of Benimaclet. (p111)

Tours & Courses

PENNY KIDD/LONELY PLANET ©

Caminart (www.caminart. es) If you understand Spanish, these themed walking tours are great, getting you deep into the art, culture and architecture of the city.

Valencia Bikes (☎650 621436; www.valenciabikes. com; Paseo de la Pechina 32; ☺9.30am-8pm) This well-established set-up runs daily three-hour guided bicycle tours in various languages, with guaranteed departures (€27.50 including rental).

Liber Tours (☎978 11 88 88; www.libertours. com; Plaza del Ayuntamiento; adult/child €22/10; ☺10.30am Mon-Sat) Recommended 2¼-hour walking tours of the centre, leaving from the town hall tourist office.

Free Tour Valencia (☎961 11 29 01; http:// freetourvalencia.com; Plaza de la Virgen; pay by donation) These English- and Spanish-language walking tours leave from the Plaza

de la Virgen; you pay what you think it's worth.

Escuela de Arroces y Paella Valenciana (☎961 04 35 40; www. escueladearrocesypaellas. com; Calle Obispo Don Jerónimo 8; €65-75) Once you know how, cooking paella isn't nearly as intimidating as you might think. So this social, fun and friendly course might be just the thing.

Poblados de la Mar (☎960 06 05 05; www. pobladosdelamar.com; walking tour €12) Informative Marga will take you for a two-hour afternoon walk around the fishing barrio of El Cabanyal, with good insights into architecture and traditional life in this intriguing part of Valencia.

Mediterranean Surf School (☎655 014250; www.mediterraneansurf school.com; La Casa de la Mar, Avenida Vicente Blasco Ibáñez Novelista 8; 2hr class from €28; ☺10am-8pm

Tue-Sun; 👫) Don't expect huge waves in Valencia, but the often-gentle swell and great weather make it a fine place to learn how to surf or paddleboard (pictured).

Horta Viva (☎691 093721; www.hortaviva. net) This company offers an excellent opportunity to visit the huerta, the area of market garden that surrounds Valencia and provides the city with its wonderful fresh produce.

València Day Tours (www.visitvalencia.com; adult/child €45/20; ☺mid-Jun Sep) In summer, a day trip to one of the towns around Valencia province leaves from the Ayuntamiento tourist office each day.

Passion Bike (☎963 91 93 37; www.passionbike.net; Calle de Serranos 16) This friendly multilingual operator offers three tours: a three-hour city tour (€25), a longer trip to La Albufera (€60) and a night tour (€20).

Four Perfect Days

Day 1

BESIDES THE OBVIOUS/SHUTTERSTOCK ©

Head first to **Mercado Central** (pictured; p54) to experience it at its most bustling, then take your time to appreciate the Gothic charms of **La Lonja** (p56). Hit **Navarro** (p41) for a rice lunch the way locals like it.

Next head to the **cathedral** (p50); check out the Holy Grail, then work off the carbs by climbing the bell tower. If you've still got energy, visit the nearby ruins of **L'Almoina** (p61).

For dinner and drinks, it has to be Russafa's enticing tapas zone. Get there early so you can browse some shops. Take your pick of the dozens of eating options that crowd these streets, then repair to **Cafe Berlin** (p97) for a cocktail.

Day 2

PUMBASTYLE/SHUTTERSTOCK ©

Head to the exhilarating **Ciudad de las Artes y las Ciencias** (p80). You may want to spend all day down here. Otherwise walk back along the riverbed-turned-park **Jardines del Turia** (pictured; p113) and dive into L'Eixample for lunch at **Las Lunas** (p88).

Sip *horchata* at lovely **Mercado de Colón** (p87) then browse the boutiques of L'Eixample towards the **Estación del Norte** (p39), another Modernista marvel.

An evening stroll through the Barrio del Carmen beckons. Stop at **Café Museu** (p76) to feel the bohemian local vibe. Dine on scrumptious tapas at **El Tap** (p73) or creative fusion at **Refugio** (p73), then hit **Jimmy Glass** (p76) for a jazzy nightcap.

Day 3

PENNY KIDD/LONELY PLANET ©

Take in the **Museo Nacional de Cerámica** (pictured; p39) and nearby **Museo del Patriarca** (p36) before the **Torres de Serranos** (p71) for grand views.

Lunch at **Lienzo** (p64) then cross to the **Museo de Bellas Artes** (p108) and spend some time with the greats of Spanish painting, including famed local artist Joaquín Sorolla.

From here, it's a short hop to **Benimaclet** (p110), where you could spend the evening in its cultural cafes. Otherwise, try one of Valencia's gastronomic restaurants – **Ricard Camarena** (p115) or Quique Dacosta's **El Poblet** (p41). Fancy a lighter meal? The same chefs run fun tapas restaurants too – **Canalla Bistro** (p100) and **Vuelve Carolina** (p42), respectively.

Day 4

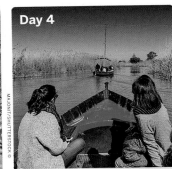

MAJONIT/SHUTTERSTOCK ©

Hire a bike and pedal out to the waterfront suburbs. Explore El Cabanyal, checking out the **Museo de Arroz** (p123) and stopping for a tapa at marvellous **Bodega Casa Montaña** (p123). Then ride or walk along the beachfront promenade. Near its northern end, **La Más Bonita** (p126) makes an appealing stop for lunch.

Next, head south out of the city to **La Albufera** (pictured; p140). Take a boat trip on the lagoon and stroll in the dunes. Watch sunset at **Mirador El Pujol**.

At night, squeeze into **Tanto Monta** (p116), then dine Moroccan in friendly, atmospheric **Balansiya** (p115). For a quiet drink head to **La Salamandra** (p117), or investigate the boisterous university nightlife nearby.

Need to Know

For detailed information, see Survival Guide (p147)

Currency
Euro (€)

Language
Spanish, Valenciano

Visas
Generally not required for stays of up to 90 days. Some nationalities will need a Schengen visa.

Money
ATMs widely available. Credit cards accepted in most hotels and restaurants.

Mobile Phones
Local SIM cards easily available. Roaming charges with an EU SIM card have been abolished.

Time
Central European Time (UTC/GMT plus one hour)

Tipping
Not widely practised; 5% is generous in a restaurant.

Daily Budget

Budget: Less than €120
Dorm bed: €15–30
Double room in a budget hotel: €60–80
Lunchtime set menu: €10–18
Bus ticket: €1.50

Midrange: €120–250
Double room in a three-star hotel: €80–120
Dinner in midrange restaurant: €35–70
Short taxi trip: €5–10

Top end: More than €250
Degustation menu in gastronomic restaurant: €80–150
Double room in an upmarket hotel: €150–250

Useful Websites

Lonely Planet (www.lonelyplanet.com/valencia) Destination information, hotel bookings, traveller forum and more.

Love Valencia (www.lovevalencia.com) Upbeat site with events and good information.

Booking.com (www.booking.com) The most useful hotel booking site for Spain.

Visit Valencia (www.visitvalencia.com) Useful official tourism site.

Renfe (www.renfe.com) Book Spanish trains.

Arriving in Valencia

The airport is an easy cab ride or metro journey from the centre, while the principal train station is fairly central.

✈ From Valencia Airport

Metro Lines 3 and 5 connect the airport, central Valencia and the port.

Taxi A taxi into the city centre costs €25 to €30 (including a supplement for journeys originating at the airport). The return journey is around €15 to €20.

🚉 From Estación Joaquín Sorolla

Bus A free shuttle bus runs the short distance to Estación del Norte, on the edge of the old town.

Taxi A taxi from here to destinations around the centre will cost €4 to €7.

Getting Around

Central Valencia is very walkable, with much pedestrianisation.

🚌 Public Transport

The integrated bus, metro and tram network is efficient, easy to use and useful.

🚲 Bike

An excellent network of bike lanes and the riverbed park give fast, traffic-free access to large parts of town. Bike hire is widespread.

🚕 Taxi

Cheap and convenient, especially into the Ciutat Vella, where there is little public transport.

🚗 Car

Impractical for a stay in the city, as well as being expensive to park.

ORISVO/SHUTTERSTOCK ©

Valencia Neighbourhoods

North Ciutat Vella (p49)
The heart of the old town is packed with character and must-see attractions.

Barrio del Carmen (p69)
Historic old-town district that's just perfect for strolling, with a bohemian vibe and good restaurants and bars.

South Ciutat Vella (p35)
The busiest part of the old town, this is a civic centre with top shopping and worthwhile attractions.

Western Valencia (p131)
An unusual zoo, a city museum and excellent parks and gardens are the highlights of this large area.

Museo de Bellas Artes

La Catedral

La Lonja

Mercado Central

Museo del Patriarca

Valencia's Seaside (p121)

A vibrant maritime quarter backs a long city beach, whose promenade offers several appealing eating and drinking options.

L'Eixample & Southern Valencia (p79)

The elegant avenues of the new town have excellent shopping and eating opportunities.

Ciudad de ◉ las Artes y las Ciencias

Northern & Eastern Valencia (p107)

Home to the city's premier art gallery and football team, and enlivened by students.

Russafa (p95)

A compact quarter bristling with intriguing tapas restaurants, quirky bars and offbeat shopping. It's a top spot for an evening out.

Explore
Valencia

El Miguelete (p53) MARCO CRUPI/SHUTTERSTOCK ©

Explore ◈
South Ciutat Vella

The southern part of the old town, centred around the sizeable town hall square, Plaza del Ayuntamiento, is a busier, more commercial area than its northern counterpart. Valencia seems a big city here, with imposing buildings, a metropolitan bustle and public institutions. The area bristles with impressive Modernista buildings, shopping is first class, and lots of accommodation choices make this many visitors' Valencia address.

The Short List

o **Museo Nacional de Cerámica (p39)** Marvelling at this stately home's exuberant blend of Modernista and baroque elements, and the impressive ceramics collection.

o **Museo del Patriarca (p36)** Admiring works by El Greco and Ribera, along with other highlights, in this seminary museum.

o **Navarro (p41)** Appreciating a perfectly prepared Valencian rice dish at this well-established restaurant.

o **Lladró (p45)** Picking your perfect porcelain at the famous Valencian ceramicists' boutique store.

o **Museo de la Seda (p39)** Learning about the silk trade from caterpillars to velvet at this handsome guild palace.

Getting There & Around

🚌 Plaza del Ayuntamiento is a major bus hub, reachable from almost anywhere in Valencia.

Ⓜ Xàtiva metro station is on the edge of the zone.

🚊 The Estación del Norte train station is right by this area.

South Ciutat Vella Map on p38

Museo Nacional de Cerámica (p39) DIGITALPEARLS/SHUTTERSTOCK ©

Top Experience 📷

Wander the Renaissance Courtyard of Museo del Patriarca

This late 16th-century seminary was founded by San Juan de Ribera, a towering Counter-Reformation figure who wielded enormous spiritual and temporal power. An impressive if austere Renaissance building, it contains a small but excellent religious-art museum. The archbishop-saint endowed it with a collection of what was then modern art.

◉ MAP P38, E1

Colegio de San Juan

📞 692 491769

www.patriarcavalencia.es

Calle de la Nave 1

admission €3

🕑 11am-1.30pm, also often 5-7pm Mon-Fri

Cloister & Chapel

The cloister-courtyard is an impressively sober Renaissance space with two levels and columns of Carrara marble. It's decorated with typically colourful tiles from Talavera. In the centre is a later statue of the sainted founder. The chapel on the right before you enter is generally shown at the end of your visit. It is dignified by tiles from Manises and Flemish tapestries. The Old Testament ceiling frescoes look a little amateurish after the splendid museum canvases.

Caravaggio

The roguish Italian master is represented here by two copies of famous works of his, presumably realised by students in his workshop. The *Judas Kiss* may have had substantial input from the master. Next to it is the larger *Crucifixion of St Peter*. One follower who learned the lessons of light and darkness particularly well was José de Ribera from nearby Xàtiva, whose chiaroscuro *Ecce Homo* here is very fine.

Thomas More

Remember *Wolf Hall*, where a doomed Sir Thomas More scribbled away in the Tower of London as he awaited his execution? It's a real thrill to see here the very manuscript More was writing, preserved in a reliquary. It's an extraordinary find, having been rediscovered here in the 1960s. He didn't finish the work, as his papers and pens were confiscated.

El Greco & Juan de Juanes

El Greco is represented here by a fabulous *Adoration,* with almost impressionistic outlines so characteristic of this painter. Another painting of St Francis and Fray León is noteworthy, too. Local boy Juan de Juanes was a deeply religious man whose biblical subjects were beautifully realised. Several of his works are here, including a fine *Epiphany* and haunting *Nazarene*.

★ Top Tips

o Though not part of the visit, it's worth also seeing the main church (at the door on the left as you face the building).

o The museum is small, so can easily be bolted onto a visit to nearby attractions such as the Museo Nacional de Cerámica (p39).

o Drop into the adjacent church to meet Lepanto, a hoary, stuffed caiman. Though legends say this was a monster that terrorised the Río Turia, it was actually a gift from the Viceroy of Peru to his uncle Juan de Ribera, the college's founder. It became a much-loved pet of the stern Catholic, who had it preserved for posterity.

✕ Take a Break

A fortifying dose of cava and some fresh oysters can be had nearby at Ostras Pedrín (p42).

La Utielana (p42) offers no-frills, typical Valencian lunch options for a pittance.

South Ciutat Vella

For reviews see
- ◎ Top Experiences p36
- ◉ Sights p39
- ✕ Eating p41
- ◻ Drinking p43
- ◻ Entertainment p43
- ◻ Shopping p43

L'EIXAMPLE

200 m
0.1 miles

N

Museo del Patriarca

Mercado Central

Biblioteca Pública de Valencia

Museo de la Seda

La Casa de los Falleros

Plaza de Tetuán
Plaza de la Reina
Plaza Redonda
Plaza del Mercado
Plaza San Agustín
Plaza del Patriarca
Plaza del Ayuntamiento
Plaza de los Pinazos

Estación del Norte

Xàtiva

C del Conde de Salvatierra
C de Sorni
C de Jorge Juan
C del Poeta Quintana
C de Pérez Bayer
C de Pizarro
C de Félix Pizcueta
C de Colón
C de Pascual y Genís
C de Correos
C de Barcas
C de Moratín
C de Garrigues
C de Padilla
C de En Sanz
C de Quevedo
C de Jesús
C de San Vicente Mártir
C del Músico Peydró
C de San Pablo
C del Arzobispo Mayoral
C de Bailén
C de Pelayo
C de Pizarro
C del Pie de la Cruz
C Guillem Sorolla
C Editor Manuel Aguilar
C del Hospital
C de Guillem de Castro

C del Marqués de Dos Aguas; Museo Nacional de Cerámica
Palacio del Marqués de Dos Aguas
C del Mar
C de la Paz
C San Andrés
C del Poeta Querol
C Virués
C Embajador Vich
C Barcelonina
C de Salvà
C de la Nave
C de las Comedias
C de Luis Adelantado
C Universidad
C del Pintor Sorolla
C Juan de Austria
C de Mosén Femades
C Roger de Lauria
C de Martínez Cubells
C Convento Santa Clara
Passeig Russafa
C Ribera
Av del Marqués de Sotelo
C del Periodista Azzati
Av María Cristina
C de San Fernando
C de Jofrens
C Trench
C San Martín
C Abadía
C Cerrajeros
Av de Alvaro Moliner
C Linterna
C del Músico Peydró

Tourist Info
Valencia
Alfonso el Magnánimo
Colón
Universidad
La Nau
Filmoteca
Ayuntamiento

Centro Cultural La Nau

Plaza de Salvà
Plaza de la Paz

Sights

Palacio del Marqués de Dos Aguas

PALACE

1 MAP P38, D1

Quite a sight from outside, this immoderate palace has a pair of wonderfully extravagant rococo caryatids curling around the main entrance. The exterior also boasts flamboyant Modernista features. The interior offers further sumptuous delights in what is now the Museo Nacional de Cerámica. (Calle del Poeta Querol 2)

Museo Nacional de Cerámica

MUSEUM

Inside the striking palace, this ceramics museum (see **1** Map p38, D1) celebrates an important local industry. Downstairs, as well as seeing a decadent hand-painted 1753 carriage, you can learn about the history of ceramics from baroque to modern, with great information (albeit sometimes a little difficult to relate to the pottery on display). Upstairs, historical ceramics are cleverly dotted with modern works, but the sumptuous, over-the-top interiors, ornate stucco, chinoiserie, damask panels and elaborate upholstery pull plenty of focus. It's an outrageous rococo extravaganza.

Look out for a fabulous painted ceiling from the original building. The modern top floor has details on ceramics production and a porcelain collection from the Alcora factory, which, along with Manises

and Paterna, was an important local production centre. Porcelain and other ceramics are still huge in the Valencian region. (📞 963 08 54 29; www.culturaydeporte.gob.es/mnescultura; Calle del Poeta Querol 2; adult/child €3/free, Sat afternoon & Sun free; ⏱10am-2pm & 4-8pm Tue-Sat, 10am-2pm Sun)

Estación del Norte

NOTABLE BUILDING

2 MAP P38, C4

Trains first chugged into this richly adorned Modernista terminal in 1917. Its main foyer is decorated with ceramic mosaics and murals – and mosaic 'bon voyage' wishes in major European languages. There's a riot of oranges and greenery outside and the wooden ticket booths inside are especially lovely. Don't miss the ceramic paintings by Gregorio Muñoz Dueñas in a room to your right. (Calle de Xàtiva; ⏱5.30am-midnight)

Museo de la Seda

MUSEUM

3 MAP P38, B2

This visually elegant modern museum makes the most of its lovely location in the 15th-century (with baroque additions) palace that was the seat of the silkmakers' guild. Silk was a major Valencian industry, and the compact, manageable display takes you through the process from caterpillars to velvet-sleeved courtiers. There are some lovely restored rooms upstairs, with the highlight being a fabulous rococo tiled floor depicting the fame of

Dressing for the Party

Valencians take Las Fallas (p114) seriously. If you want to know how seriously, head to **La Casa de los Falleros** (Albaes; Map p38, B3; ☑963 52 14 00; www.lacasadelos falleros.com; Calle de Quevedo 6; ⏱9.30am-1.30pm & 4.30-8pm Mon-Fri, 10am-2pm & 4.30-8pm Sat, closed Sat afternoon Jul & Aug). Here's the place to buy a traditional *fallera* dress and accessories for the fiesta, or to simply see roll upon roll of embroidered, sequined cloth and racks of off-the-peg dresses. Check your credit-worthiness; a ready-made ensemble can cost over €500, while made-to-measure starts well into four figures. Another central shop stocking Fallas materials is **Álvaro Moliner** (Map p38, C2; ☑963 51 41 90; www.alvaro moliner.com; Pasaje de Ripalda 18, Calle de Moratín; ⏱10am-1.30pm & 4.30-8.30pm Mon-Fri).

silk, here in a woman's form, across four continents represented by geographically relevant beasts.

There's also a loom (active for group visits) and very pleasant patio with a restaurant. (Colegio del Arte Mayor de la Seda; ☑697 155299; www.museodelasedavalencia.com; Calle del Hospital 7; adult/child incl San Nicolás €7/free; ⏱10am-7pm Tue-Sat, 10am-3pm Sun & Mon)

Ayuntamiento

MUSEUM

4 MAP P38, C3

Valencia's handsome neoclassical town hall dominates the square that takes its name. Within is the **Museo Histórico Municipal**, a repository of items important to the city's identity, such as the sword that Jaime I reputedly brandished when defeating the Muslim occupiers, the flag they surrendered with, the Moorish keys to the city and a fascinating 1704 map of Valencia. You can also explore the chandeliered grandeur of the function rooms and enjoy the view from the balcony. (Town Hall; ☑962 08 11 81; www. valencia.es; Plaza del Ayuntamiento 1; admission free; ⏱9am-1.45pm Mon-Fri)

Luis Adelantado

GALLERY

5 ◉ MAP P38, E1

This stylish spot is a local reference point for high-quality, carefully selected contemporary art exhibitions. There are often some real gems on display, and younger artists are given an annual showcase exhibition. (☑963 51 01 79; www. luisadelantado.com; Calle de Bonaire 6; admission free; ⏱10am-2pm & 4-8pm Mon-Fri, by appointment Sat)

Centro Cultural La Nau

UNIVERSITY

6 ◉ MAP P38, E2

Long the headquarters of the University of Valencia, with a harmonious cloister-courtyard that's worth popping into. It's lined with plaques of notable academics, and nearby are the old library and the Sala Estudi General exhibition space. (☎963 86 43 77; www. uv.es; Calle de la Nave; ⊙10am-2pm & 4-8pm Tue-Sat, 10am-2pm Sun Sep-Jul, 10am-2pm Tue-Sun Aug)

Biblioteca Pública de Valencia LIBRARY

 7 ◉ MAP P38, A2

Obscured by palm trees in the gardens of a former psychiatric hospital, the city's main public library is in a grand 16th-century building. The Gothic entrance is original and the open atrium space on the ground floor showcases an impressive domed ceiling. Flooded with natural light, the library has photo and art exhibitions and is a cool spot to beat the heat. The few English books available are for young learners of the language. (☎962 56 41 30; www.bibliotecas publicas.es/valencia; Calle del Hospital 13; admission free; ⊙9am-8.30pm Mon-Fri Sep-Jul, to 2pm Aug)

Eating

Navarro VALENCIAN €€

 8 ✖ MAP P38, C3

A byword in the city for decades for its quality rice dishes, Navarro is run by the grandkids of the original founders and it offers plenty of choice, outdoor seating and helpful service. (☎963 52 96 23; www.restaurantenavarro.com; Calle del Arzobispo Mayoral 5; rice dishes €15-18; ⊙1-4pm Mon-Sat; 🛜)

El Poblet GASTRONOMY €€€

 9 ✖ MAP P38, D3

This upstairs restaurant, overseen by famed Quique Dacosta and with Luis Valls as chef, offers elegance and fine gastronomic dining at prices that are very competitive for this quality. Modern French and Spanish influences combine to create sumptuous degustation menus. Some of the imaginative presentation has to be seen to be believed, and staff are genuinely welcoming and helpful. (☎961 11 11 06; www.elpobletrestaurante. com; Calle de Correos 8; degustation menus €85-125; ⊙1.30-2.30pm & 8.30-10pm Mon & Wed-Fri, 8.30-10pm Sat; 🛜)

Centro Cultural La Nau

Vuelve Carolina MEDITERRANEAN €€

Overseen from a distance by noted chef Quique Dacosta, this upbeat bar-restaurant (see 9 Map p38, D3) offers style – those clothes-horse bar stools could be more comfy though – and an inspiring selection of tapas and fuller plates. These range from exquisite Peruvian-influenced creations to tacos, rices and more. Service is solicitous, and watching the open kitchen under the benevolent gaze of cardboard deer heads is always entertaining. (963 21 86 86; www. vuelvecarolina.com; Calle de Correos 8; tapas €6-24; 1.30-3.45pm & 8.30-10-30pm Mon-Thu, 1.30-4pm & 8.30-11pm Fri & Sat;)

El Encuentro SPANISH €€

10 MAP P38, C2

There's a very likeable old-fashioned feel about this place, which offers stalwart Spanish cuisine at fair prices. Expect plenty of stew-type dishes, such as beans and chorizo; the meat and fish plates are also reliable. Browse the wines on your way in so you don't have to get up again. The pleasant summer terrace is set back from the street. (963 94 36 12; www.restauranteelencuentro.es; Calle de San Vicente Mártir 28; mains €10-18; 1.30-4.30pm & 8.30pm-12.30am Mon-Sat;)

La Utielana VALENCIAN €

11 MAP P38, D2

Not the easiest to track down, tucked-away La Utielana well merits a minute or two of sleuthing. Very Valencian, it packs in the crowds, drawn by the wholesome fare and exceptional value for money. (963 52 94 14; Calle de San Andrés 3; mains €6-11; 1.15-4pm & 8.30-10.30pm Mon-Fri, 1.15-4pm Sat)

Ostras Pedrín SEAFOOD €€

12 MAP P38, E2

With white tiles and a simple backstreet vibe, this pleasing little place serves up different varieties of oysters, freshly shucked to order. You can have them grilled or in tempura as well, but they're great fresh, accompanied by a glass of cava, white wine or vermouth. (963 76 70 54; www. facebook.com/ostraspedrinbar; Calle de Bonaire 23; oysters €2.30-5.20; 11am-midnight Mon-Sat, 11am-4pm Sun)

Al Adwaq NORTH AFRICAN €

13 MAP P38, E2

This is the pick of a few North African restaurants in these narrow streets, and its corner vibe with exposed brick is very inviting. The aromas alone might induce you to enter. It's delicious homestyle Moroccan fare, with a few eastern-Mediterranean-style dishes, too. No alcohol is served. (963 44 02 35; www.aladwaq.com; Calle de la Nave 16; dishes €5-12; 1.30-4.30pm & 8.30-11.30pm Mon-Sat)

Drinking

Lotelito
COCKTAIL BAR

14 🍸 MAP P38, D2

The smooth industrial decor, moody lighting and motivated staff make this bar-restaurant-cafe a fine venue for a pre-dance-floor or post-dinner drink. A range of spirits in a wire cage towers high over the bar, and mixed drinks are well prepared. The pleasant outdoor seating makes it a good venue for breakfast or lunch, too. (📞963 06 78 52; www.lotelitovalencia.com; Calle de Barcas 13; 🕐8am-1.30am; 📶)

Entertainment

Teatro Principal
THEATRE

15 ⭐ MAP P38, D2

One of Valencia's main venues for theatre, dating from the mid-19th century, with varied programming. (📞963 53 92 60; http://teatres.gva.es; Calle de Barcas 15; 🕐Sep-Jun)

Shopping

Cestería El Globo
ARTS & CRAFTS

16 🔒 MAP P38, C2

In business since 1856, this charming shop features piles of traditional wickerwork – how about a basket for your bicycle? – plus rocking horses and other solid wooden toys. (📞963 52 64 15; www.facebook.com/cesteriaelglobo; Calle del Músico Peydró 16; 🕐9.45am-1.30pm & 4.30-8pm Mon-Fri, 10am-2pm & 5-8.15pm Sat)

Cut-Price Cinema

A Valencia classic is the **Filmoteca** (Map p38, C2; 📞963 53 93 00; www.ivac.gva.es/la-filmoteca; Plaza del Ayuntamiento), a cinema in the Teatro Rialto building that screens undubbed classic and art-house films for a pittance (€2.50). It's so cheap that you might find a couple of people have just paid for a comfy place for a snooze.

Sombreros Albero
HATS

17 🔒 MAP P38, D4

For any of your hat needs, head to this venerable concern near the Estación del Norte, run by the Albero family since 1820. Many are made by the family, and the range of berets, trilbies, cowboy hats and more is impressive. There's another store, the original, near the Mercado Central. (📞963 51 22 45; www.sombrerosalbero.es; Calle de Xàtiva 21; 🕐10am-2pm & 4.30-9pm Mon-Sat May-Sep, 10am-2pm & 5-8.30pm Mon-Sat Oct-Apr)

Las Ollas de Hierro
ARTS & CRAFTS

18 🔒 MAP P38, C1

Valencia's oldest shop dates from the late 18th century and has an intriguing history and loads of character. Its souvenir cards, Las Fallas accessories and religious items are eclipsed by its wonderful range of figures and landscapes for Christmas Nativity scenes. (☏963 92 20 24; Calle de los Derechos 4; ⏱9.30am-1.30pm & 4.30-8pm Mon-Fri, 10am-2pm & 5-8pm Sat, closed Sat afternoon May-Oct)

Galería 4 ART

19 🔒 MAP P38, E2

This attractive little gallery and framing shop makes for a pleasant browse and is a good spot to pick up a piece of Valencian modern art. (☏963 51 00 63; www.galeriacuatro.es; Calle de la Nave 25; ⏱10am-2pm & 5-8.30pm Mon-Sat, closed Sat Jun-Oct)

Devil Records MUSIC

20 🔒 MAP P38, C1

This central, well-established little music shop deals mostly

in new and used vinyl, with rock predominant. A great spot for a look around. The street is called Manyans in Valenciano. (☏963 92 03 38; Calle de Cerrajeros 5; ⏱11am-2pm & 5-8.30pm Mon-Sat)

Turrones Ramos FOOD

21 🔒 MAP P38, C1

One of the Valencian region's most famous products is *turrón*, a sweet almond-based nougat that comes in soft or hard versions and is a traditional staple of Christmas eating across Spain. Enjoy it year-round in this shop from one of the most famous producers. (☏963 92 33 98; www.turrones-ramos.es; Calle Sombrerería 11; ⏱10am-2pm & 5-8pm Mon-Fri, 10am-2pm Sat)

Plaza Redonda

SILVIA J/SHUTTERSTOCK ©

Plaza Redonda

ARTS & CRAFTS

22 🔒 MAP P38, C1

This circular 19th-century space in the heart of town – once the abattoir of Valencia's Mercado Central – is ringed by stalls. Though it feels a little overly touristy after an elaborate makeover, there are a couple of very worthwhile shops selling traditional ceramics. (⏲ hours vary)

Lladró

CERAMICS

23 🔒 MAP P38, D2

More than 50 years ago, three Lladró brothers produced the first of their famed porcelain sculptures. Today, their factory on the city's northern outskirts employs hundreds of people and exports its figurines worldwide. Its retail outlet is deliberately sited on Valencia's smartest street. In what is almost a mini-museum, you can browse among and purchase its winsome figurines. (✆ 963 51 16 25; www. lladro.com; Calle del Poeta Querol 9; ⏲ 10am-8pm Mon-Sat, to 2pm Sat Aug)

Valencia Club de Fútbol Megastore

SPORTS & OUTDOORS

24 🔒 MAP P38, C3

Right on Plaza del Ayuntamiento, this sizeable shop offers souvenirs, scarves, woolly hats and many a memento of the city's major football club. There's even a cafebar on the top floor. (✆ 963 51 47

Designer Corner

Calle del Poeta Querol and adjoining Calle de Salvá are where wealthy Valencians drop by for a bit of high-end shopping. Big-name designers and emblematic brands have their boutiques here.

42; http://vcfshop.com; Avenida del Marqués de Sotelo 1; ⏲ 10am-10pm Mon-Sat, 11am-8pm Sun)

Oxfam Intermón

CLOTHING

25 🔒 MAP P38, D1

Oxfam's flagship shops in Spain are a long way from the charity-shop aesthetic. This is one of the best, featuring stylish clothing from sustainable materials as well as other fair-traded products and artworks. (✆ 963 52 76 44; www. oxfamintermon.org; Calle del Marqués de Dos Aguas 5; ⏲ 10am-2pm & 5.30-8.30pm Mon-Sat)

Librería Patagonia

BOOKS

26 🔒 MAP P38, B2

Excellent travel bookshop and travel agency with some guides in English and lots of Lonely Planet titles. There's a great selection of maps and hiking-related books and items too. (✆ 963 93 60 52; www.libreriapatagonia.com; Calle del Hospital 1; ⏲ 9.30am-2pm & 4.30-8pm Mon-Fri, 10.30am-2pm & 5-8pm Sat)

Walking Tour 🥾

The Centro Histórico

This whistle-stop walk takes you past the historic quarter's major sights and monuments plus a selection of other intriguing buildings. It includes both the north and south of the old town, and a jaunt through the characterful Barrio del Carmen. Designed as a getting-your-bearings stroll, it could easily take a day or two if you explore all the sights.

Start Plaza del Ayuntamiento

Finish Plaza de la Reina

Length 2.7km; one hour

🚌 Numerous buses terminate in Plaza del Ayuntamiento.

Ⓜ Xàtiva is a short stroll away.

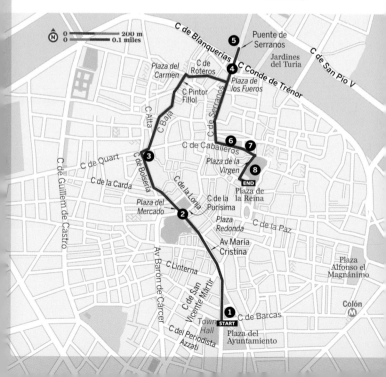

❶ Plaza del Ayuntamiento

Plaza del Ayuntamiento is flanked by noble civic buildings, including the **town hall** (p40). It's the civic centre of Valencia and entrance hall to the historic city, a long, busy plaza narrowing towards the north; an arrow pointing into the heart of the medieval town.

❷ Mercado Central & La Lonja

Take the left fork from the plaza up Avenida María Cristina. Two of Valencia's principal buildings face each other across this road. The **Mercado Central** (p54) is a glorious Modernista building that's the city's main market, while **La Lonja** (p56), a Gothic masterpiece, was also once used by the merchants of the city for trading goods.

❸ Plaza del Tossal

Continue up Calle de Bolsería to reach **Plaza del Tossal**. This landmark square is the meeting of many ways, one of which is Calle Baja, an important medieval thoroughfare that snakes its way into the heart of Barrio del Carmen, in the northwest of the old town.

❹ Torres de Serranos

Calle Baja becomes Calle Pintor Fillol and will lead you to the Plaza del Carmen, overlooked by the church of the same name. From here, take Calle de Roteros – which harbours a couple of excellent tapas options – eastwards to the imposing **Torres de Serranos** (p71), once a major gateway in the city walls but now free-standing.

❺ Jardines del Turia

Beyond the gate, cross onto Puente de Serranos, the bridge leading to the city's northern region. It's a bridge over a river that no longer exists: the Turia was diverted in the 20th century and its former watercourse is now a fabulous stretch of **park** (p113).

❻ Calle de Caballeros

Retrace your steps through the gate and head down characterful Calle de Serranos to Calle de Caballeros. The latter was medieval Valencia's main street and is lined with palaces and mansions. This bit is dominated by the **Palau de la Generalitat** (p62).

❼ Plaza de la Virgen

Emerge at **Plaza de la Virgen** (p61), a wide square with a famous fountain and a major city church. This is where Valencians gather in the evening and 'meet me by the fountain' is the standard beginning to a night out with friends around here.

❽ Catedral de Valencia

From here, head southwards until you reach Plaza de la Reina, where you'll see the entrance to the **cathedral** (p50) overlooked by the emblematic **Miguelete** (p53) bell tower.

Explore ◈

North Ciutat Vella

The heart of historic Valencia, this area contains several of the city's key sights and is many visitors' first port of call when exploring town. The cathedral's treasures include the Holy Grail, while the magnificent Lonja is one of the great Gothic civil buildings. Other remnants of the city's storied past are scattered throughout the area, where the vibrant Mercado Central is one of Spain's most striking and best market halls.

The Short List

○ **La Lonja (p56)** Feeling ennobled by the majesty of the principal hall at this sumptuous civil Gothic masterpiece.

○ **Mercado Central (p54)** Working up a serious hunger by examining the quality produce at this beautiful market hall.

○ **La Catedral (p50)** Clapping your eyes on nothing less than the Holy Grail, and trudging up the spiral stairs of the emblematic bell tower for unmatched views.

○ **Iglesia de San Nicolás (p61)** Admiring the fabulously restored painted ceiling at this tucked-away gem of a church.

Getting There & Around

🚌 Though most of the area is effectively pedestrianised, many buses, including 4, 8, 9 and 11, pass through Plaza de la Reina in front of the cathedral.

Ⓜ The closest stations to the area are Alameda and Pont de Fusta, across the Turia riverbed.

North Ciutat Vella Map on p60

La Catedral (p50) SERGIO FORMOSO/GETTY IMAGES ©

Top Experience 📷
Find the Holy Grail at La Catedral

The centrepiece of Valencia's old town, the cathedral is a noteworthy sight and an intriguing place to visit, not least because it harbours nothing less than what's said to be the Holy Grail. It's a fairly low-slung building in truth, and impresses much more from within than without, though its soaring bell tower is a city icon.

👁 MAP P60, D3

📞 963 91 81 27

http://museocatedral
valencia.com

Plaza de la Reina

adult/child/family
€8/5.50/18

🕐 10.30am-5.30pm or
6.30pm Mon-Sat

Interior

Built over the city mosque, which had itself been built over a Visigothic church, after the 13th-century reconquest, the church's interior is low but spacious and atmospheric. The main structure is Gothic, while the side chapels with their neoclassical Corinthian columns are mainly from an 18th-century renovation. The undecorated capitals and unadorned brick give the nave a somewhat austere feel.

The Crossing

The most visually rewarding part of the cathedral, the crossing is topped by a picturesque octagonal tower instead of the more customary dome. It features two tiers of arches – noteworthy structures with alabaster windows, built in the 14th and 15th centuries. Over the altarpiece, vibrant Renaissance frescoes, recently rediscovered under posterior baroque adornment, feature angels against a blue and starry background. Don't miss the 14th-century Gothic pulpit, from which it is said local favourite San Vicente Ferrer preached. His portrait hangs above.

The Renaissance paintings stand out amid the baroque adornment and, though now incomplete, feature 12 musical angels acclaiming the Assumption. By comparison, the gilt cherubs, red marble and corkscrew columns seem like extravagant style over substance.

The walnut choir stalls are more quality Renaissance work, as is the altarpiece, with beautifully restored paintings of biblical scenes.

Ambulatory

The 15th-century alabaster sculpture of the Virgin, known as *La Virgen del Coro*, is much revered locally. Pregnant women pray to her and walk nine times around the cathedral to ensure a successful carriage and delivery.

★ Top Tips

o The cathedral also opens on Sunday afternoons from 2pm to 5.30pm or 6.30pm between March and November.

o Most shops and several key sights in Valencia close for a few hours mid-afternoon, but the cathedral stays open, making this a good time to visit.

o Be aware that women outside the cathedral often try to force a sprig of 'lucky' rosemary on you, for which they'll then try to charge you a ridiculous amount.

✗ Take a Break

The restaurants immediately surrounding the cathedral are mostly mediocre tourist traps. Head to La Salvaora (p63) for quality modern Spanish or Delicat (p63) for exquisite tapas.

Opposite, directly behind the altar, the Capilla de la Resurrección has a polished alabaster portico, a relief of the Resurrection and the spooky left arm of San Vicente Mártir, with ringed fingers and the odd hair still seemingly in place. Nearby, the fine late Gothic altarpiece in the Capilla de San Dionisio y Santa Margarita is a work of Vicente Macip.

Capilla de San Francisco de Borja

The aristocratic 16th-century Francisco de Borja, an important noble, had a rapid change of life when his wife died. He entered the Jesuit order – the altar painting in this side chapel depicts the moment. The two paintings that flank it are by Goya (1789) and show the duke bidding farewell to his family as he enters the holy life, and his intervention to save an unconfessed dying man. Picturesque lurking demons – prefiguring Goya's black paintings – are thwarted in their little scheme to whisk the sinner downstairs.

Other Chapels

Things to look out for in other chapels around the nave include six canvases of the life of Mary in the Capilla de San Pedro, painted by Nicolás Falcó, and Pedro de Orrente's impressive chiaroscuro San Sebastián in the chapel of the same name.

El Miguelete

Museum

The cathedral **museum** (incl in cathedral entry, €3 when cathedral visits closed; ⏱10am-6.30pm Mon-Sat year-round, 2-6.30pm Sun Jun-Sep, 10am-2pm Sun Mar-May & Oct, closed Sun Nov-Feb) is a good-looking blend of the modern and venerable. There are some excellent religious paintings here – it is intriguing to see the huge evolution in style in just one generation between the Renaissance paintings of Vicente Macip and those of his son, the great Juan de Juanes. The highlights, though, are the wonderful 14th-century carved apostles, precursors of those that flank the cathedral's main door. In the basement you can view Roman and medieval remains.

Capilla del Santo Cáliz

This high star-vaulted chamber, built in the 14th century as a chapterhouse, is a square space that apparently holds – suspension of disbelief alert – nothing less than the Holy Grail itself, housed within a magnificent late Gothic alabaster screen, formerly the entrance to the choir. The 12 reliefs are early Renaissance works – the Old Testament below, and the New above. The cup itself is an agate vessel dating from the 1st century BCE, so at least the date is right. It has medieval handles and an interesting history.

The Water Court

As it has done for over 1000 years, the Tribunal de las Aguas (Water Court) meets every Thursday at noon outside the cathedral's Puerta de los Apóstoles. Here, Europe's oldest legal institution settles local farmers' irrigation disputes. The eight tribunal members in their black peasant smocks each represent one of the main water channels that irrigate the rich, fertile agricultural land around Valencia. The exclusively oral proceedings take place in Valenciano, and fines are expressed in lliures, a long-defunct local currency. In reality, there are rarely any complaints and it's all slightly anticlimactic.

El Miguelete

Started in the 17th century, the cathedral's **bell tower** (Torre del Micalet; adult/child €2/1; ⏱10am-7pm Apr-Oct, 10am-6.30pm Mon-Fri, 10am-7pm Sat, 10am-1pm & 5.30-7pm Sun Nov-Mar) is an emblem of the city. Its 207 chunky spiral stairs lead you to unparalleled views over the historic centre. Interestingly, the perimeter and height are exactly equal at a tick under 51m. The 14 bells ring out for masses and weddings but formerly warned of corsair attacks.

Top Experience 📷

Sip Wine and Watch the Bustle in Mercado Central

What's glorious about Valencia's central market, apart from its striking early 20th-century architecture, is its ordinariness: although it's on a larger, more impressive scale, its rows of meat, fish and vegetable stalls are very typical of market halls in any traditional town or barrio in Spain. The quality and presentation are sky-high though, and the sheer spectacle merits a visit.

◉ MAP P60, B4

📞 963 82 91 00

www.mercadocentral valencia.es

Plaza del Mercado

🕑 7.30am-3pm Mon-Sat

Seafood

For many, the most spectacular counters are in the seafood section. There are cephalopods aplenty, crustaceans galore and fish of all kinds – it's a good moment to bone up on some restaurant menu vocabulary. El Galet is a classic stall that specialises in live eels.

Deli Stalls

An abundance of cured meats and cheeses projects an almost idealised version of Spain. Sliced small goods are vacuum-packed in a moment and their ultra-slim packing profile should satisfy carry-on requirements for even the most demanding of budget airlines. Many will arrange delivery around Europe too.

Fruit & Vegetables

The pride of Valencia is its *huerta,* the market-garden area surrounding the city that produces crops galore on rich alluvial soil. A brief gaze at the plump tomatoes on display here invokes a notion of pure goodness.

Central Bar

The best way to absorb the market ambience after a spell of browsing the aisles is to sit down with a glass of wine or cup of coffee in hand. The double-countered bar is stylish and turns out tasty tapas (dishes €10 to €16, daily roll €5.80), but you'll likely need to queue. Its name misleads: you'll find it at the western end.

Palanca

The undisputed monarch of the meat section, this centenarian butcher has some magnificent cuts on offer. Admire the premium sides of beef and *buey* (ox, but actually usually older cows) in the glass-paned freezer alongside.

★ Top Tips

○ Be sensitive. Stall-holders gain nothing from tourists gazing at their produce, so if you're not buying, give priority to local customers and ask politely before taking photos.

○ If you want something vacuum-packed, ask for *'envasado al vacío'.*

✖ Take a Break

The bar in the market itself is the place to grab a pew, a wine and a tapa while watching the action.

Just up the road, La Sénia (p64) does all-day tapas with a market-based focus.

Top Experience 📷

Check Out the Door of Sin at La Lonja

This splendid building, a Unesco World Heritage site, was originally the city's silk and commodity exchange, built in the late 15th century when Valencia was booming. It's one of Spain's finest examples of a civil Gothic building, designed by the architect Pere Compte, who was obviously at the peak of his powers. Two main buildings flank a citrus-studded courtyard.

◎ MAP P60, C3

📞 962 08 41 53

www.valencia.es

Calle de la Lonja

adult/child €2/1, Sun free

🕙10am-7pm Mon-Sat, to 2pm Sun

Audio Guide

There's very little printed information around the site, so the audio guide (€3) is a good investment. It also includes information on the building's exterior, which is well worth examining, perhaps before you start the visit of the interior.

Puerta de los Pecados

The 'door of sin' was meant to send a powerful message to merchants entering the Sala de Contratación beyond about the dangers of sharp practice (we could do with a few more doorways like this today). The wide portal is decorated with tendrils and figures on both sides. They merit a much closer look: some of the symbolism is obscure, but there are some very comical scenes. Look out for slapstick battles with beasts, drunkenness, lust, an eagle nipping someone's undercarriage and two men defecating into bowls held by a woman – perhaps representing fertility and nature's cycle of regeneration.

Sala de Contratación

Utterly magnificent, this imposing space has twisted columns ascending 17m to the star-vaulted ceiling, huge church-like Gothic windows with intricate tracery, and a real sense of majesty. Here silk and wool were traded and banking was done – it's a veritable cathedral of commerce. The design was daringly modern for its time. The inscription around the wall is motivational, suggesting that good mercantile conduct is a sure path to heaven. Don't miss the lovely restored doorway leading to a spiral staircase.

Consulado del Mar

The main building opposite the entrance was where a tribunal sat to discuss maritime

★ Top Tips

○ Groups commonly visit, but are whisked through very quickly, so it's worth waiting in the courtyard if you want to enjoy the key rooms in relative silence.

○ The Lonja is one of the municipal museums on a combined ticket – worth the €6 investment if you'll be visiting a few.

✕ Take A Break

If you're visiting in the late afternoon or at a weekend, seek out nearby Tyris on Tap (p65) for a delicious craft beer in contrastingly modern surroundings.

Need a fishy snack? The famous sardines at no-frills Tasca Ángel (p63) are just around the corner.

mercantile issues. It's a solid structure crowned by merlons, below which is a superbly realised Renaissance loggia, a frieze of kings and mythical figures, and shields of Valencia. Inside are two noteworthy halls and, downstairs, a crypt-like space.

Ground Floor

The ground-floor chamber of the Consulado del Mar is notable for a fine Renaissance ceiling and panels of Jaime I, San Vicente Ferrer and a guardian angel made using the local *socarrat* technique, involving the application of pigment to lime-coated dry brick. There's a video here with background. On your way in here from the Sala de Contratación, look right for a saucy relief of the Devil indecently assaulting an animal with a pair of bellows.

Sala Dorada

The top floor of the Consulado del Mar building, behind the Renaissance loggia, is known as the

The Ratpenat

If you want a 'respect' animal to stick on your coat of arms, you'd think you could do a bit better than a bat. But there it is right on Valencia's, and the Ratpenat (*valenciano:* bat) is the symbol of the city. Though there are the usual spurious tales about its arrival on the town shield, the most likely is that it gradually evolved from a *vibra,* a female dragon figure common in popular mythology and tradition in this part of the Mediterranean.

'Golden Hall' for its chief feature: a noble *artesonado* (decorated wooden ceiling), brought here from the former town hall. It's a stunning gilded and coloured piece of work from the early 15th century, almost nail-free, with scenes of music and battle between the beams, prophets and mythical scenes on the upper supports, and humans, flora and fauna on the lower ones.

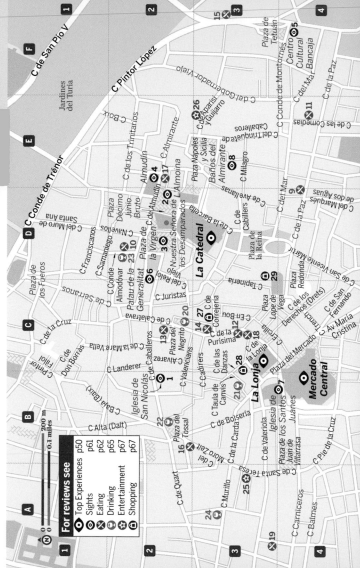

North Ciutat Vella

C de San Pio V

F

C Pintor López

Jardines del Turia

E

C Conde de Trénor

D

C

B

A

1

Plaza de Tetuán

Centro Cultural ⊙5

Plaza del Mar Bancaja

C del Mar

C de la Paz

×15

3

4

C de las Comedias ×11

C del Gobernador Viejo

C de Montornés

C Conde de Montornés

⊙26 C de Aparisi y Guijarro

C del Trinquete de Caballeros

Plaza Nápoles y Sicilia

Baños del Almirante

C Milagro

⊙8

C de Avellanas

C del Mar

C del Marqués de dos Aguas

×9

C de los Trinitarios

Almudín

C Boix

C de los Trinitarios

×17 ⊙4

C del Almudín

C Almirante

Plaza Décimo Junio Bruto

C Navellos

C del Muro de Santa Ana

×23 ⊙10

C Samaniego

Almodóvar

Palau de la Generalitat

C Conde Almodóvar

C Franciscanos

Plaza de la Virgen ⊙3

Nuestra Señora de los Desamparados

C de Caballers

C de la Barcella

La Catedral ⊙

Plaza de la Reina

C de la Paz

Plaza de San Vicente Mártir

C de San Vicente Mártir

⊙6 C del Reloj Viejo

C Juristas

Plaza de los Fueros

C de Serranos

C de la Cruz

C de Don Borrás

C de Cajatrava

×13 C de la Mare Vella

C del Negrito ⊙20

⊙29

Plaza Redonda

C de Tapinería

C Tapinería

Plaza de Lope de Vega

C de los Derechos (Drets)

C de San Fernando

Av María Cristina

C Trench

C Pintor Fillol

C Baja (Baix)

C Alta (Dalt)

Iglesia de San Nicolás

C Landerer

C de Caballeros

⊙1

C Valencians

C Cadirers

C Correjería

×14 27×

×12

C de la Purísima

C En Bou

×28

⊙21

La Lonja ⊙

C de la Lonja

Plaza del Mercado

Mercado Central ⊙

×22 Plaza del Tossal

C del Moro Zeit ×16

C de Bolsería

C de la Carda

C de Valeriola

Iglesia de los Santos Juanes ⊙7

Plaza de los Santos Juan de Villarrasa

C de Quart

C Murillo

C de Santa Teresa

×24

×25

C de Pie de la Cruz

C Carniceros

C Balmes

×19

1

2

3

4

```
For reviews see
⊙ Top Experiences    p50
⊙ Sights             p61
✕ Eating             p62
✕ Drinking           p65
🏠 Entertainment      p67
🏠 Shopping           p67
```

200 m
0.1 miles

N

Sights

Iglesia de San Nicolás   CHURCH

1 ⊙ MAP P60, B2

Reopened to the public after a magnificent restoration, this single-naved church down a passageway is striking. Over the original Gothic vaulting, the ceiling is a painted baroque riot. The altarpiece is in similar style, with corkscrew (Solomonic) columns framing the twin saints who share the church: San Nicolás saving boys from the pickling tub, and San Pedro Mártir with a cutlass in his head. (☏ 963 91 33 17; www.sannicolasvalencia.com; Calle de Caballeros 35; adult/child incl Museo de la Seda €7/free; ⊙ 10.30am-7.30pm Tue-Fri, 10.30am-6.30pm Sat, 1-8pm Sun Oct-Jun, 10.30am-9pm Tue-Fri, 10.30am-7.30pm Sat, 11.30am-9pm Sun Jul-Sep)

L'Almoina   RUINS

2 ⊙ MAP P60, D2

Beneath the square just east of Valencia's cathedral, the archaeological remains of the kernel of Roman, Visigoth and Islamic Valencia shimmer through a water-covered glass canopy. Head downstairs for an impressively excavated, atmospheric melange of Roman baths, forum buildings and a factory, as well as bits of the Moorish *alcázar* (fortress) and a royal cemetery. Later remains come from a building erected on this square as a hospital for the poor. (☏ 962 08 41 73; www.valencia.es; Plaza Décimo Junio Bruto; adult/child €2/1, Sun free; ⊙ 10am-7pm Mon-Sat, to 2pm Sun)

Plaza de la Virgen   SQUARE

3 ⊙ MAP P60, D2

This busy plaza, ringed by cafes and imposing public buildings, was once the forum of Roman Valencia. The reclining figure in its central fountain represents the Río Turia, while the eight maidens with their gushing pots symbolise the main irrigation canals flowing from it.

Almudín   HISTORIC BUILDING

4 ⊙ MAP P60, E2

The 15th-century Almudín originally served as the city's granary, storing wheat brought in from the surrounding countryside. Writing high up on the interior walls indicates the level each year's grain reached and where it was harvested. The lofty arched hall is now used for art exhibitions, though paintings often seem dwarfed by the building's grandeur. (L'Almodí; ☏ 962 08 45 21; Calle de Almudin; adult/child €2/1, Sun free; ⊙ 10am-2pm & 3-7pm Tue-Sat, 10am-2pm Sun)

Centro Cultural Bancaja   ARTS CENTRE

5 ⊙ MAP P60, F4

High-quality temporary art exhibitions, often featuring major international names, are the main offering at this bank-run centre, which also has other cultural events. (☏ 960 64 58 40; www.fundacion bancaja.es; Plaza de Tetuán 23; admission free; ⊙ 10am-2pm Mon, 10am-2pm & 4-8pm Tue-Sun)

Iglesia de San Nicolás (p61)

the Mercado Central is gradually being restored. The notable ceiling fresco is being put back in place using digital technology and an old photo. The interior is Italianate baroque, despite the building's 13th-century origins. The audio guide, narrated by the church itself, is entertaining despite a few reminders of eternal judgement. (☑963 58 49 82; www.mentavalencia. com; Plaza del Mercado; adult/child €7/free incl Museo de la Seda, €10/free adding San Nicolás; ☉10am-7.30pm Mon-Sat, 1-7.30pm Sun)

Baños del Almirante
HISTORIC BUILDING

8 MAP P60, E3

These Arab-style baths, constructed in 1313, functioned continuously as public bathing facilities until 1959. It's worth dropping in if you're passing by. Strategically placed buckets and piped sounds of water add a little atmosphere, but it could do with more information. Nevertheless, it's a pretty spot. (www.valencia.es; Calle Baños del Almirante 3-5; admission free; ☉10am-6pm Tue-Fri, 9am-2pm Sat & Sun)

Palau de la Generalitat
PALACE

6 MAP P60, D2

This handsome 15th-century Gothic palace, much amended over the years, is the seat of government for the Valencia region. Its symmetry is recent: the original Renaissance tower received its twin only in the 1950s. Free guided tours can be booked by telephone. (☑963 42 46 36; www.valencia.es; Calle de Caballeros 2; ☉tours 9am-2pm Mon-Fri)

Iglesia de los Santos Juanes
CHURCH

7 MAP P60, B4

Heavily damaged when set ablaze by anticlerical mobs during the Spanish Civil War, this locally important church next to

Eating

Entrevins
SPANISH €€€

9 MAP P60, D4

With a quiet, restrained elegance, this upstairs restaurant makes a lovely lunchtime retreat from the bustle of the street and is handy for several nearby sights. Grab a window table to watch the passers-by below and enjoy the seriously tasty food. The lunchtime set menu (€22, weekdays only) is top value for this quality and includes two shared starters. (☏963 33 35 23; www.entrevins.es; Calle de la Paz 7; mains €20-27; ☉1.30-3.30pm & 8.30-11pm Tue-Sat)

Delicat · TAPAS €€

10 🍴 MAP P60, D2

At this friendly, intimate option, the open kitchen offers an unbeatable-value set menu of samplers for lunch (€14.50) and delicious tapas choices for dinner. The decor isn't lavish but the food is memorable, with a range of influences at play. It's best to book ahead as the small space fills fast. (☏963 92 33 57; Calle Conde Almodóvar 4; dishes €8-18; ☉1.45-3.30pm & 8.45-11.30pm Tue-Sat, 1.45-3.30pm Sun; 🛜)

Cinnamon · FUSION €€

11 🍴 MAP P60, E4

This intimate space is so tiny, you wonder how it prepares anything more elaborate than a fried egg. But wonders emerge from the open kitchen in dishes bursting with taste and freshness. Creative plates include the crunchy house salad, a fab daily special and good options for vegetarians. A very worthwhile dining experience, if there's room. (☏963 15 48 90; Calle de las Comedias 5; dishes €8-14; ☉1.30-4pm Mon, 1.30-4pm & 8.30-11pm Tue-Sat; 🛜🍴)

Tasca Ángel · TAPAS €

12 🍴 MAP P60, C3

This no-frills place has been in business for 75 years and is famous for its fishy tapas, but in particular grilled sardines, which are fresh and delicious, with a great hit of garlic and salt. Order them with a cold beer or white wine and find inner peace. (☏963 91 78 35; Calle de la Purísima 1; sardines €4; ☉10.30am-3pm & 7-11pm Mon-Sat)

La Salvaora · SPANISH €€

13 🍴 MAP P60, C2

Refined, elegant but not expensive, this intimate spot is decorated with

The Patron of the City

The **Real Basílica de Nuestra Señora de los Desamparados** (Map p60, D2; www.basilicades amparados.org; Plaza de la Virgen; ☉7.30am-2pm & 4.30-9pm) is Valencia's central spot for active Christianity. There's serious modern Catholicism at work here in the circular baroque space, with South American priests giving almost-nonstop services to parishioners, and a payment kiosk for dedicated masses. The focus: a highly venerated statue of the Virgin of the Abandoned, patron of Valencia. Due to her slightly inclined pose, she's affectionately nicknamed La Jorobadita (the Hunchback).

black-and-white portraits of flamenco stars. At first, the menu of Spanish favourites – which beef cheek, bull tail, ham, croquettes – looks familiar, but modern presentation and exquisite quality soon prove this is no ordinary *tasca* (tapas bar). Exceptional value for this standard; the tapas degustation menu (€32) is a steal. (🔊963 92 14 84; www.lasalvaora.com; Calle de Calatrava 19; mains €13-19; ☺8.30-11pm Jun-Aug, 1.30-3.30pm Wed, 1.30-3.30pm & 8.30pm-midnight Thu-Mon Sep-May)

El Patio de Pepa
TAPAS €

14 ✕ MAP P60, C3

This tiny tapas joint is extremely cosy, with well-thought-out decor and fresh produce bursting from the bar. Everything is cooked fresh and delicious, especially the skewers, and service is very cordial. (🔊960 61 97 90; www.facebook.com/elpatiodepepa; Calle de la Purísima 6; tapas €4-14; ☺noon-4pm & 7pm-midnight, closed Tue & Wed Jul & Aug)

Lienzo
GASTRONOMY €€€

15 ✕ MAP P60, F3

This modishly styled white-and-grey dining room sees some wonderful things done with seafood in particular. Lienzo means canvas, and there's certainly an artistic flourish to the presentation. Consistent quality is produced across the various tasting menus (€32 to €65), which are the best way to experience the place. (🔊963 52 10 81; www.restaurantelienzo.com; Plaza de Tetuán 18; mains €21-29; ☺1.30-

3.30pm & 8.30-10.30pm Mon-Sat, 1.30-4pm Sun)

La Pilareta
TAPAS €

16 ✕ MAP P60, B2

Earthy, a century old and barely changed, La Pilareta is great for hearty tapas and *clóchinas* (small, juicy local mussels), available between May and August. For the rest of the year it serves *mejillones* (mussels), altogether fatter if less tasty. A platterful comes in a spicy broth that you scoop up with a spare shell. It's got atmosphere in spades. (Bar Pilar; 🔊963 91 04 97; www.barlapilareta.es; Calle del Moro Zeit 13; mussels €7.10; ☺noon-midnight)

Bar Almudín
TAPAS €€

17 ✕ MAP P60, E2

Sweet, cosy and good-humoured, Almudín combines fresh produce from Valencian market gardens with conserves to produce fine tapas dishes. Try the delicious *escalivada* (cold grilled vegetable medley); otherwise a set menu is top value for €17.50, with a vegetarian version available. Behind the bar, the attractive shelves stock a particularly good variety of vermouth. Tables outside are great in summer. (🔊963 52 54 78; Calle de Almudín 14; tapas €6-16; ☺12.30-11.30pm Wed-Mon)

La Sénia
TAPAS €€

18 ✕ MAP P60, C3

This casual and cordial all-day option run by a Spanish-Italian couple does an appropriately tasty line in flavoursome Mediterranean cuisine, with a short menu based on fresh produce and quality conserves. Try the tomatoes topped with bonito... delicious! (📞611 497677; www.taberna lasenia.es; Calle de la Sénia 2; tapas €4-14; ⏰noon-midnight)

Ligazón

GALICIAN €€

19 MAP P60, A3

In a pleasantly quiet corner of the old town, far from the tourist beat, this welcoming place does really good Galician-style octopus with *pimentón* (paprika) and boiled potatoes. There is also excellent steak and fish on offer, plus bargain lunch and breakfast deals. (📞961 14 11 12; www.facebook.com/pulperialigazon; Calle Arolas 11; mains €11-21; ⏰8am-5pm Mon-Fri, 11am-5pm Sat, 8-11.30pm Thu-Sat)

Drinking

Café Negrito

BAR

20 MAP P60, C2

Something of a local legend, this cafe-bar on a little old-town square has an intellectual, socially aware, left-wing clientele and art exhibitions often focused on sustainable development or NGOs. The large terrace is a top spot to while away an evening. (📞963 91 42 33; www. facebook.com/CafeNegritoValencia; Plaza del Negrito; ⏰4pm-4am; 📶)

Tyris on Tap

MICROBREWERY

21 MAP P60, B3

This outlet for a local microbrewery has 10 taps issuing some pretty tasty craft beers by the pint and half-pint. There's one of our

Café de las Horas (p66)

The Local Tongue

Valencia has two official languages: Spanish (*español* or *castellano*) and *valenciano*. Almost everyone is at ease speaking Spanish and increasing numbers of Valencians – particularly younger ones, who've studied it as a compulsory subject in school – handle the local language comfortably as well.

According to linguists and certainly for a traveller's purposes, the regional language is a form of Catalan, a language shared with Catalonia, Andorra and the Balearic Islands (though many locals don't like to see it as such). But the linguistic dimension is only one of many and language is always an emotive issue. The fallout over the Catalan independence issue makes this even more of a hot potato.

In Valencia, there's a constant to-and-fro as councils replace Spanish street names with the *valenciano* equivalents, then their successors change them back. The result is a little chaotic: some streets have a different name at each end. While the difference between the two versions is often minimal, it can still cause confusion. Occasionally we use the *valenciano* form where it's clearly the dominant one, or the official one in the case of places such as Russafa (Ruzafa). However, since Spanish is the version the majority uses, we've elected to stick with it in most cases.

favourite central terraces out front to enjoy it, and some simple bar food such as nachos to soak it up. You can book a Saturday tour of the brewery via the website or by phone. (📞 961 13 28 73, tours 📞 961 06 40 50; www.cervezatyris.com; Calle Taula de Canvis 6; ⏱6.30pm-1am Tue-Sun; 📶)

Sant Jaume
BAR, CAFE

22 🚇 MAP P60, B2

This tiny former pharmacy is a haunt for local characters, and features a marble counter and ornate embossed wooden ceiling. It's a sound stop for a coffee or beer any time of day; it also does a very decent *agua de Valencia* (cava and orange-juice cocktail). For elbow room and people-watching, head to the outdoor tables. (📞 963 91 24 01; www.cafesantjaumevalencia.com; Calle de Caballeros 51; ⏱noon-1.30am; 📶)

Café de las Horas
BAR

23 🚇 MAP P60, D2

Offers high baroque, tapestries, music of all genres, candelabras, bouquets of fresh flowers and a long list of exotic cocktails, pictured, as well as themed Sunday brunches (11am to 4pm). Service could improve but it's always an intriguing place to stop for a coffee or a *copa* (mixed drink). (📞 963 91 73 36; www.cafedelashoras.com; Calle Conde Almodóvar 1; ⏱10am-2am; 📶)

Beat Brew Bar COFFEE

24 MAP P60, A3

The friendly couple who run this speciality coffee and tea bar will happily talk you through the multitude of options available from their laboratory-like set-up. Whatever you choose will be fair trade and organic. Plant-based milk available only. (☏603 296760; http://beatbrewbar.com; Calle Murillo 22; ☺9.30am-5.30pm Thu-Tue)

Entertainment

Radio City LIVE PERFORMANCE

25 ⭐ MAP P60, A3

Almost as much a mini cultural centre as a club, Radio City, which fills up from around 1am, pulls in the punters with activities such as a language exchange, and DJs or live music every night. There's everything from flamenco to funk; check the website for what's on. (☏963 91 41 51; www.radiocityvalencia.es; Calle de Santa Teresa 19; ☺10.30pm-4am, opens earlier for some events)

Espacio Inestable DANCE

26 ⭐ MAP P60, E3

This edgy space presents innovative movement and dance of sometimes spectacular quality. It's a notable reference point of Valencia's alternative cultural scene. Check its website for upcoming shows, which normally run over a weekend. (☏963 91 95 50; www.espacioinestable.com; Calle de Aparisi y Guijarro 7; tickets €5-10)

Shopping

Bodegas Baviera WINE

27 MAP P60, C3

This excellent wine shop has reasonably priced reds and whites from all over the country, as well as some interesting spirits, olive oils and sherries. The musician owner, Vicente, has worked in the trade for decades and is quite a character. (☏963 91 80 60; http://bodegasbaviera.es; Calle de Correjería 40; ☺10am-2pm & 6-9pm)

Madame Bugalú FASHION & ACCESSORIES

28 MAP P60, C3

Madame Bugalú and her killer poodle, to give the shop its full name. Stylish and fairly pricey by Spanish standards, it offers original, striking clothing and accessories for women. Just down the road at Calle de la Lonja 6, sibling store Bugalú has fashion for both men and women. (☏963 15 44 76; www.facebook.com/bugaluvalencia; Calle de las Danzas 3; ☺10am-2pm & 5-8.30pm Mon-Sat)

Artesanía Yuste CERAMICS

29 MAP P60, D3

This lovely shop, tucked away in a central location, has an excellent array of colourful ceramics, with some particularly fine tiles made with the *socarrat* technique. It's run by a second-generation ceramicist, whom you can sometimes watch at work. (☏630 373603; Plaza del Miracle del Mocadoret 5; ☺10am-2pm & 4.30-7.30pm Mon-Fri, 10am-2pm Sat)

Explore 🧭

Barrio del Carmen

The northwest corner of the old town is Valencia's oldest quarter, offering bohemian local character and several good museums. El Carme, as it is known in valenciano, is fertile ground for eating and drinking, with a fine selection of little bars and restaurants to track down in its narrow, confusing medieval street plan. Try to visit the barrio (district) twice: once during the week, when you'll see quiet streetscapes with local residents going about their business, and once on a weekend evening, when it fills with Valencians seeking out restaurants and bars.

The Short List

○ **Torres de Quart (p71)** *Gazing in awe at this imposing city gate and climbing it for great views over the old town and riverbed.*

○ **Institut Valencià d'Art Modern (p71)** *Discovering the sublime sculptures of Julio González in this airy contemporary gallery.*

○ **Jimmy Glass (p76)** *Swaying to the sounds of quality jazz at this iconic venue.*

○ **Refugio (p73)** *Experiencing one of the barrio's many backstreet foodie spots, which combines a typical Carmen bohemian vibe with quality cuisine.*

Getting There & Around

🚶 The essentially pedestrianised Barrio del Carmen is best accessed on foot.

🚌 Buses running along the Turia can drop you at the edge of the *barrio*. Bus 5 runs along the *barrio's* western and northern edges.

🚗 If you're staying in the *barrio*, you can enter in a vehicle.

Barrio del Carmen Map on p70

Torres de Quart (p71) VITALYEDUSH/ISTOCK EDITORIAL/GETTY IMAGES ©

Barrio del Carmen

For reviews see

◉	Sights	p71
✕	Eating	p73
🍷	Drinking	p76
🛍	Shopping	p77

200 m
0.1 miles

Puente de las Artes

Paseo de la Pechina

Institut Valencià d'Art Modern

◉ 2

Museu de Prehistoria

Museu de Etnologia

◉ 4

◉ 8

✕ 15

C de Corona

Puente de San José

C de Blanquerías

C de Salvador Giner

◉ 5   Convent Carmen

✕ 13

Centro del Carmen

Café Museu

◉ 6

✕ 14

C del Museo

C de Na Jordana

C de Liria

C de Beneficencia

C del Dr Chiarri

C Ripalda

C de San Ramón

Museo de Prehistoria

C de Pintor Zariñena

C de Dr Beltrán Bigorra

C del Pintor Zariñena

Torres de Quart

◉ 1

C de Guillem de Castro

C de Pinzón

Plaza del Tossal

C de Bolsería

🍷 18   🍷 11

Plaza Vicente Iborra

Plaza del Músico López Chavarri

✕ 19

Plaza de Mossén Sorell

✕ 10   C de Santo Tomás

C Alta (Dalt)

🛍 23

C Raga

✕ 22

🍷 16

C Baja (Baix)

C Mirto

Plaza del Carmen

Plaza del Árbol

C Pintor Fillol

C de Padre Huérfanos

Jardines del Turia

Torres de Serranos

Museo del Corpus

◉ 3

Plaza de los Fueros

✕ 12   🍷 21   ◉ 9   C de Roteros

C Roda

C de Serranos

C Franciscanos

C del Muro de Santa Ana

C Conde de Trénor

Puente de Serranos

Pont de Fusta

C de los Trinitarios

Plaza Décimo Junio Bruto

C de Almudín

Plaza de la Virgen

C Navellos

C Samaniego

Conde Almodóvar

C Juristas

C Cocinas

C de la Cruz

🍷 17

C de la Mare Vella

C de Caballeros

L'Iber ◉ 7

🍷 24

C Valencians

C de Cadirers

C de Calatrava

C Alvarez

C Landerer

C de Don Borrás

C del Moro Zeit

F

E

D

C

B

A

1

2

3

4

N

Sights

Torres de Quart GATE

1 MAP P70, A4

Spain's most magnificent city gate is quite a sight from the new town. You can clamber to the top of the 15th-century structure, which faces towards Madrid and the setting sun. Up high, notice the pockmarks caused by French cannonballs during the 19th-century Napoleonic invasion. (☏618 803907; www.valencia.es; Calle de Guillem de Castro; adult/child €2/1, Sun free; ☉10am-7pm Tue-Sat, to 2pm Sun)

Institut Valencià d'Art Modern GALLERY

2 MAP P70, B2

This impressive gallery hosts excellent temporary exhibitions and owns a small but impressive collection of 20th-century Spanish art. The most reliably permanent exhibition on display is the Julio González collection. This Catalan sculptor (1876–1942) lived in Paris and produced exquisite work with iron that influenced later artists such as David Smith and Eduardo Chillida.

The González collection was a major reason for the gallery's creation and there are some great pieces here – the series of sensitive iron *Masques* are exquisite – and they are beautifully lit and displayed. Along with some classical nudes and busts in bronze, plaster, terracotta and stone, his offbeat iron forms are very much of his time and are sometimes reminiscent of the painted works of Picasso. The modest scale of González' pieces prefigures more monumental works later in the 20th century. The gallery's cafe makes a pleasant spot for a drink. (IVAM; ☏963 17 66 00; www.ivam.es; Calle de Guillem de Castro 118; adult/child €6/3, Sun free; ☉11am-7.30pm Tue-Thu, Sat & Sun, to 9pm Fri)

Torres de Serranos GATE

3 MAP P70, E2

Once the main exit to Barcelona and the north, the imposing 14th-century Torres de Serranos overlook the former bed of the Río Turia. Together with the Torres de Quart, they are all that remain of Valencia's old city walls. Climb to the top for a great overview of the Barrio del Carmen and riverbed. (☏963 91 90 70; www.valencia.es; Plaza de los Fueros; adult/child €2/1, Sun free; ☉10am-7pm Mon-Sat, to 2pm Sun)

Museo de Etnología MUSEUM

4 MAP P70, A3

This ethnographic display shares the halls with the archaeological museum in the Beneficència cultural complex (p73). The recently renovated display focuses on four rural environment types as well as the city. (☏963 88 35 65; www.letno.es; Calle de Corona 36; with Museo de Prehistoria adult/child €2/1, free weekends; ☉10am-8pm Tue-Sun)

IMAGE: DAVID MARIN FOTO/SHUTTERSTOCK ©

Institut Valencià d'Art Modern (p71)

Convent Carmen CULTURAL CENTRE

5 ◉ MAP P70, C1

In the grounds and church of a former convent, this casual cultural space hosts everything from music and movies to yoga and debates. In the large garden, street food is served from converted shipping containers. (http://conventcarmen. com; Plaza Portal Nou 6; ⊙noon-1am Wed-Sat, from 6pm Wed-Fri summer)

Centro del Carmen CULTURAL CENTRE

6 ◉ MAP P70, D2

Behind the church on the landmark Plaza del Carmen, this centre occupies the handsome Gothic cloister and rooms of the monastery that once backed it. It's in a fairly severe Cistercian style and devoted to temporary exhibitions; there are usually several on at a time. It's worth a visit for a stroll around the cloister alone. (☏963 15 20 24; www.consorciomuseos.gva. es; Calle del Museo 2; admission free; ⊙11am-7pm Tue-Sun Oct–mid-Jun, to 9pm mid-Jun–Sep)

L'Iber MUSEUM

7 ◉ MAP P70, D4

With more than 95,000 pieces on display and over a million in total, L'Iber, set in a historic palace, claims to be the world's largest collection of toy soldiers. The huge 4.7m x 2.8m set piece of the Battle of Almansa (1707), a key encounter in the War of the Spanish Succession, has 9000 combatants, while other dioramas and cases teem with battalions and regiments from antiquity to modern times and even a little science fiction. (Museo de Soldaditos de Plomo; ☑963 91 86 75; www.museoliber.org; Calle de Caballeros 22; adult/under 27yr €8/5; ⊙11am-2pm & 4-7pm Sat, 11am-2pm Sun Sep-Jun, 11am-2pm & 4-7pm Wed-Sun Jul & Aug)

Museo de Prehistoria   MUSEUM

8 ◉ MAP P70, B3

This perhaps overly comprehensive museum of archaeology has some excellent pieces and loads of interesting information, but pick and choose or you'll be overwhelmed by the rows of flint tools and potsherds. No bone or stone is left unturned. Part of **La Beneficència** (☑963 88 35 65; www.labeneficencia. es; admission free; ⊙10am-8pm Tue-Sun) cultural complex, it's particularly strong on cave art and pre-Roman Iberian culture. Info is in *valenciano* and Spanish, but printed sheets in English fill in some gaps. Sections on the Romans and ancient money are more modern in style. (www.museuprehistoriavalencia. es; Calle de Corona 36; with Museo de Etnología adult/child €2/1, free weekends; ⊙10am-8pm Tue-Sun)

Eating

El Tap   TAPAS, VALENCIAN €€

9 ✖ MAP P70, E2

Tap is one of Barrio del Carmen's rich selection of small, characterful restaurants and is genuinely welcoming. The food is market-based and originally and delightfully

prepared. Dishes with local tomatoes are a standout, and there's a carefully chosen list of both wines and boutique beers. Excellent value. (☑963 91 26 27; www.facebook.com/restauranteeltapvalencia; Calle de Roteros 9; mains €10-18; ⊙7.30-11.30pm Mon-Fri, 1.30-3.30pm & 7.30-11.30pm Sat; 🛜)

Refugio   FUSION €€

10 ✖ MAP P70, C3

Named for the civil-war hideout opposite and simply decorated

---

Corpus Christi Procession

Corpus Christi is a major Valencian festival, celebrated with an elaborate procession, symbolic traditional dances and mystery plays on the ninth Sunday after Easter (ie three days after the feast of Corpus Christi itself). The procession was first held in 1355 and **Museo del Corpus** (Casa de las Rocas; Map p70, E2; ☑963 15 31 56; www.valencia.es; Calle de Roteros 3; admission free; ⊙10am-2pm & 3-7pm Tue-Sat, 10am-2pm Sun) is the place to investigate it. Behind tall doors rest Las Rocas, giant carts, their paintwork darkened with age, that are wheeled out on the day. The earliest of them dates back to the 16th century. Upstairs the fancy costumes and props that feature in the procession are displayed.

Paella & Other Rice Dishes

There's something life-affirming about a proper paella, but there's more to this most Valencian of dishes than meets the eye.

Types of Rice Dish

There's a whole world of rices in Valencia. Paella has all the liquid evaporated, *meloso* rices are wet, and *caldoso* rices come with broth. Rices reflect the seasons, with winter and summer ingredients making their way into the dish depending on the month. Almost any ingredient can be used, including all types of vegetables, fish, seafood and meat.

Paellas are typical of the Valencian coast. Meat paellas normally have chicken and rabbit, with green beans and other vegetables in summer, or perhaps fava beans and artichokes in winter. Fish rices tend to be served more liquid, with calamari or cuttlefish supplying the flavour and prawns or langoustines for decoration. If you add prawns to a meat paella, it's a *paella mixta. Arroz negro* (black rice) is another typical coastal rice that's made with squid ink and fish stock. *Fideuà* is similar, but made with fine pasta. Fresh rockfish are used to make a fish stock. *Fideuà* is quicker to cook, as the noodles are done faster than rice. Popular seafood-based winter rices include a cauliflower and salt-cod paella.

Secrets of the Rice

The base always includes short-grain rice, garlic, olive oil and saffron. The best rice is *bomba,* which opens accordion-like when cooked, allowing for maximum absorption while remaining firm. Paella should be cooked in a large shallow pan to enable maximum contact with flavour. And for the final touch of authenticity, the grains on the bottom (and only those) should form a crunchy, savoury crust known as the *socarrat.*

Tips on Ordering

For Valencians, rice is exclusively a lunchtime dish, though a few places do prepare it at dinnertime for the tourist trade. Restaurants should take around 20 minutes or more to prepare a rice dish – beware if they don't – so expect to wait. You'll need two people or more to order a rice dish à la carte. You can phone restaurants ahead to order your rice dish so you don't have to wait. On weekends, heading to the beach, into the *huerta* or to Albufera villages such as Pinedo or El Palmar to eat rice dishes is a local tradition, but Valencians also love to get together at someone's house and cook up a rice dish themselves.

in whitewashed brick, Refugio preserves some of the Carmen *barrio's* former revolutionary spirit. Excellent Med-fusion cuisine is presented in lunchtime menus of surprising quality: there are some stellar plates on show, though the veggie options aren't always quite as flavoursome. Evening dining is high quality and innovative. Warm and welcoming. (🕿 690 617018; www.refugiorestaurante.com; Calle Alta 42; mains €14-23, set menu €15-18; 🕑 2-4pm & 9-11.30pm; 🛜)

L'Ostrería del Carme   SEAFOOD €

This little stall inside the Mossén Sorell market (see 19 🅰 Map p70, C3) is a cordial spot and a fabulous snack stop. It has oysters of excellent quality from Valencia and elsewhere; sit down with a glass of white wine and let them shuck you a few. (🕿 629 145026; www.laostreriadelcarmen.com; Plaza de Mossén Sorell; oysters €3-4; 🕑 11am-3pm Mon-Sat & 5-8.30pm Thu & Fri)

El Celler del Tossal   VALENCIAN €€

11 🍴 MAP P70, C4

This intimate, elegant, two-level spot is a cut above the many tourist-focused eateries in this zone. At last research, it had been taken over by an enthusiastic young chef couple who were doing a delicious line in quality mains involving seafood, duck and more, as well as exquisite desserts. Classy sommelier service adds to the experience. (🕿 963 91 59 13; www.elcellerdeltossal.com; Calle de Quart 2; mains €16-26;

🕑 1.30-3.30pm Mon & Wed, 1.30-3.30pm & 8.30-10.30pm Thu-Sun)

Mattilda   FUSION €€

12 🍴 MAP P70, D2

The decor here is stylish, modern and unpretentious, much like the team, who offer friendly service, an imaginative à la carte selection and a good-value lunch menu (€12). Portions are small but tasty. (🕿 963 92 31 68; Calle de Roteros 21; mains €12-18; 🕑 2-4pm Mon & Tue, 2-4pm & 9-11.45pm Wed-Sat; 🛜)

La Tastaolletes   VEGETARIAN €

13 🍴 MAP P70, C1

La Tastaolletes does a creative range of vegetarian tapas and mains. Pleasantly informal, it serves good, wholesome food created from quality ingredients. Salads are large and leafy, and desserts (indulge in the cheesecake with stewed fruits) are a dream. There's a daily lunch for €12 and outdoor seating. (🕿 963 92 18 62; www.latastaolletes.es; Calle de Salvador Giner 6; mains €7-10; 🕑 1.30-4pm & 8-11.30pm Tue-Sat, 1.30-4pm Sun, evenings only Aug; 🛜✍)

Yuso   VALENCIAN €€

14 🍴 MAP P70, D2

In a strategic location with outdoor tables on the Plaza del Carmen, this popular spot is an expansion from the original tucked-away weekend-only location nearby. It does a range of good-value set menus, including at nighttime, that always include rice or *fideuà*.

Café Museu

A real forum for bohemian souls in the Carmen district, **Café Museu** (Map p70, C2; 📞960 72 50 47; Calle del Museo 7; ⏱9am-11pm Tue-Thu, to 1.30am Fri, 11am-1.30am Sat, 11am-11pm Sun, from 6pm Aug; 🛜) is a grungy, edgy spot that has an impressive cultural program including English–Spanish conversation sessions, regular live music, theatre and more. The terrace is a popular place to knock back a few beers.

The quality is solid rather than spectacular but it's definitely good value. (📞963 92 24 48; www.restaurantesyuso.com; Plaza del Carmen 6; mains €10-16; ⏱1-4pm & 8pm-midnight; 🛜)

La Lluna

VEGETARIAN €

15 🍴 MAP P70, B3

Friendly and full of regulars, with walls of clashing tilework, La Lluna has been serving quality, reasonably priced vegetarian fare (including a superb-value, four-course lunch menu for €8.50) for over 30 years. You can check what's cooking that day on its Facebook page. There's outdoor seating on the quiet pedestrian street. (📞963 92 21 46; www.restaurante-lalluna.com; Calle de San Ramón 23; mains €6-8; ⏱9am-4pm & 8-11.30pm Mon-Sat; 🛜✏)

Drinking

Jimmy Glass

LIVE MUSIC

16 🍺 MAP P70, C3

Atmospheric Jimmy Glass is just what a jazz bar should be, with dim lighting and high-octane cocktails. It has four live performances a week, many of them free, and runs an annual jazz festival in October/November that attracts some top musicians. At other times it plays tracks from the owner's vast CD collection. Tapas are available Thursday to Saturday. (www.jimmyglassjazz.net; Calle Baja 28; ⏱8pm-2.30am Mon-Thu, 9pm-3.30am Fri & Sat; 🛜)

L'Ermità

BAR

17 🍺 MAP P70, D3

On a very central backstreet, this is a top option for a drink, with decent music, regular cultural events, a friendly crowd of regulars and cordial staff. The quirky interior is comfortably cosy but can overheat: the streetside tables are prime territory on a warm night. (📞963 91 67 59; www.facebook.com/lermitacafe; Calle Obispo Don Jerónimo 4; ⏱7pm-1.30am Mon-Fri, noon-1.30am Sat & Sun)

Trapezzio

BAR, GAY

18 🍺 MAP P70, C4

On a typically grungy Barrio del Carmen square, this well-established cafe and bar has a very mixed, bohemian clientele and is an important fixture in the local gay scene. It's got a great terrace where you can kick back with a drink. (📞623 103862; www.facebook.com/trapezzio; Plaza del Músico López Chavarri 2; 🕑9am-2am Mon-Fri, 6pm-2am Sat & Sun; 🛜)

Shopping

Mercado de Mossén Sorell   MARKET

19 🔒 MAP P70, C3

This petite and luminous market occupies an interesting part of the Barrio del Carmen. A facelift has left it looking lovely, and it's a great destination for gourmet bites. There's a sweet little tapas scene here, with folk downing oysters or trying wines. (Plaza de Mossén Sorell; 🕑7.30am-3pm Mon-Sat, plus 5-8.30pm Thu & Fri Sep-Jul)

Pángala   FASHION & ACCESSORIES

20 🔒 MAP P70, C2

This lovely shop does a great line in 'slow bags' that are made by hand in a relaxed manner. They are all unique and there are other items such as storage baskets. There's a dedicated 'vegan' line with no animal products used. (📞676 094782; www.pangala.es; Calle Na Jordana 2; 🕑11am-2pm & 5.30-8.30pm Tue-Sat)

Al Vent   JEWELLERY

21 🔒 MAP P70, D2

Original, beautiful and compassionately priced jewellery and other creations from silver and more. Pass through the floral arch into the attractive interior, where

staff are super-friendly, making it an ideal stop for a hand-luggage-friendly gift for someone back home. There's another outlet at Calle Calatrava 4. (📞623 178181; www.alvent.com; Calle de Roteros 17; 🕑10.30am-9.30pm)

Pannonica   VINTAGE

22 🔒 MAP P70, C3

A quirky and intriguing shop selling vintage objects, furniture and other curiosities. It's a pleasurable, friendly trap for anyone with a retro bent. (📞696 951055; www.facebook.com/Ajazzevintage; Calle Baja 28; 🕑11.30am-2pm & 5.30-9pm Mon-Fri, 11.30am-3pm Sat)

Santo Spirito Vintage   VINTAGE

23 🔒 MAP P70, C3

In the heart of the Carmen, this is one of Valencia's better vintage shops, featuring a great array of classic leisurewear and denim. It's a pleasant change to have plenty of room to move and browse too. (📞961 14 63 44; www.santospiritovintage.com; Calle Alta 22; 🕑11am-2pm & 5-9pm Mon-Sat)

Luna Nera   FASHION & ACCESSORIES

24 🔒 MAP P70, D4

This original and atmospheric store sells colourful alternative and vintage-styled clothing and accessories for women. There's always some interesting new arrivals, and prices are reasonable. (www.facebook.com/lunaneravalencia; Calle de Caballeros 16; 🕑10.30am-2.30pm & 5-10pm)

Explore ◈

L'Eixample & Southern Valencia

L'Eixample, or El Ensanche, means 'the expansion', and was developed once Valencia got too big for its old walled town. Laid out in the 19th century, it's a zone of elegant streets and wide avenues, replete with upmarket shopping and eating options. In the south of this area are the otherworldly buildings of the fabulous Ciudad de las Artes y las Ciencias, one of Valencia's major highlights.

The Short List

○ **Ciudad de las Artes y las Ciencias (p80)** Gazing in awe at a majestic assemblage of modern architecture.

○ **Mercado de Colón (p87)** Seeing and being seen at this Modernista market, now full of eateries and delis.

○ **Abanicos Carbonell (p92)** Becoming a fan of hand-powered cooling at this venerable fan shop.

○ **Palau de les Arts Reina Sofía (p92)** Listening to a soaring aria in the mothership-has-landed surrounds of this futuristic concert hall.

○ **L'Umbracle Terraza (p91)** Dancing the summer nights away in a spectacular open-air setting.

Getting There & Around

🚌 Lines crisscross the area, with Gran Vía del Marqués del Turia a major thoroughfare.

Ⓜ Colón station is handiest for the shopping district. Xàtiva station puts you at the area's northwestern edge.

🚶 North L'Eixample is in easy walking distance of the old town, but the Ciudad de las Artes y las Ciencias is a 3km walk.

L'Eixample & Southern Valencia Map on p86

Ciudad de las Artes y las Ciencas (p80)
ARCHITECT: SANTIAGO CALATRAVA; IMAGE: DAVID C TOMLINSON/GETTY IMAGES ©

Top Experience 📷
Attend a Concert in the Ciudad de las Artes y las Ciencias

This aesthetically stunning complex occupies a massive 350,000-sq-metre swath of the old Turia riverbed. It's mostly the work of world-famous, locally born architect Santiago Calatrava. He's a controversial figure for many Valencians for running over budget and various design issues. Nevertheless, it's awe-inspiring stuff, and pleasingly family oriented.

👁 MAP P86, B2

City of Arts & Sciences
📞 961 97 46 86
www.cac.es
Avenida del Professor López Piñero

Palau de les Arts Reina Sofía

Brooding over the riverbed like a giant beetle, its shell shimmering with translucent mosaic tiles – the cause of quite a few problems – this ultramodern **arts complex** (tours ☎672 062523; www.lesarts.com; Avenida del Professor López Piñero 1; guided visit adult/child €11/8.80; ⏱guided visits 11am, 12.15pm, 1.30pm, 3.45pm & 5pm), pictured, has four auditoria and enticing levels of plants poking out from under the ceramic exoskeleton. Unless you have tickets for a performance, a guided tour is the only way to enter. Tours run five times daily in Spanish and English: book online.

Booking for performances in advance online can get you big discounts at the Palau de les Arts. What's more, any unsold seats are sold at 50% below the starting price from two hours (one hour at weekends) before the curtain rises.

Hemisfèric

The unblinking eye of the **Hemisfèric** (Map p86, B1; ☎961 97 46 86; www.cac.es; sessions adult/child €8/6.20, incl Museo de las Ciencias Príncipe Felipe €12/9.30; ⏱from 10am) is at once planetarium, IMAX cinema and laser show. Sessions are roughly hourly, with a break at lunchtime, and multilingual soundtracks are available. Book ahead in summer, as it has limited capacity and often fills up.

Museo de las Ciencias Príncipe Felipe

This brilliant **science museum** (☎961 97 47 86; www.cac.es; adult/child €8/6.20, with Hemisfèric €12/9.30; ⏱10am-6pm or 7pm mid-Sep–Jun, 10am-9pm Jul–mid-Sep; 👪), stretching like a giant whale skeleton, has a huge range of interactive material covering everything from outer space to brain biology. It goes into detail on its themes, incorporating issues like the environment and nailing that elusive concept of learning for fun. All info is available in English.

★ **Top Tips**

o Many hotels in Valencia offer weekend packages that include entry to attractions at the Ciudad de las Artes y las Ciencias: this can be a handy deal.

o Ticket queues for the Oceanogràfic (p87) can be long: avoid them by booking online or buying tickets at the desk of the nearby Museo de las Ciencias Príncipe Felipe, where lines are invariably shorter.

✗ **Take a Break**

There are mediocre catering outlets dotted around the complex and a good restaurant, Contrapunto, in the Palau de les Arts. There's also a knot of eateries along nearby Avenida Instituto Obrero de Valencia, including excellent seafood at Sólo del Mar (p88).

Calatrava: Valencia's Controversial Architect

Santiago Calatrava, the world-famous Valencian architect responsible for most of the Ciudad de las Artes y las Ciencias, is a mercurial talent renowned for his public projects such as bridges, stations, museums and stadiums – creations experienced by thousands of people every day.

You'll recognise his grand-scale structures immediately, his signature as distinctive as the Coca-Cola logo. Technologically, he pushes to the limits what can balance, counter, take and impart stress in concrete, iron and steel. For Valencia, Calatrava is as significant as Gaudí remains for Barcelona. The Catalan's use of *trencadí* (slivers of broken-tile mosaic) and his fluid forms based upon nature have been a major influence upon his Valencian successor. Calatrava's soaring structures, all sinuous white curves with scarcely a right angle in sight, also relate to things organic: the vast blinking eye of the Hemisfèric or the filigree struts, like veins on a leaf, of the Umbracle, a vast, shaded walkway in the Ciudad de las Artes y las Ciencias. Most of the complex is Calatrava's design and it's an unforgettable testimony to his talent and vision. Make a point, too, of dropping beneath the Puente de la Exposición in the centre of town to the Alameda metro station with its soaring struts and bold curves. Calatrava felt that making public spaces beautiful was forgotten about in a post-war Europe bent on rapid, economical reconstruction of shattered cities and has sought to change that perception. His works glorify numerous Spanish cities and metropolises all over the world.

So, Santiago is a local hero then? Not quite. Calatrava has been criticised by some in the city for significant budget overruns and structural issues with some of his projects. The Palau de les Arts went €45 million over budget and has had structural problems, the Ágora took years to complete, and the road safety of the Assut d'Or bridge that spans the complex has been criticised. Many of his more recent projects in other countries have also gone vastly over budget, and several have had to be halted because the funds dried up. They look brilliant, though, and a few generations from now the cost may be forgotten.

Umbracle

This 320m-long portal to the complex (pictured) unifies the buildings and contains the car park and offices. Atop it, under a feathery ribbed roof, is an area of garden that becomes a glitzy bar (p91) on summer evenings, while downstairs is a fancy *discoteca* (nightclub).

Ágora

Poking out of the ground like a giant purple mussel, Ágora is a versatile exhibition space that has hosted art showings and tennis tournaments, but has a whiff of white elephant about it.

Walking Tour 🚶

Modernisme Meander

This walk takes in Valencia's main Modernista buildings. While Barcelona was the capital of this Catalan architectural style that flourished in the late 19th and early 20th centuries, Valencia was definitely in second place. Numerous buildings in the centre of the city are stunning examples of Modernisme, while so many others wink at it, with an unexpected flourish enlivening otherwise sober lines.

Start/Finish Mercado Central

Length 3.25km; 1½ hours

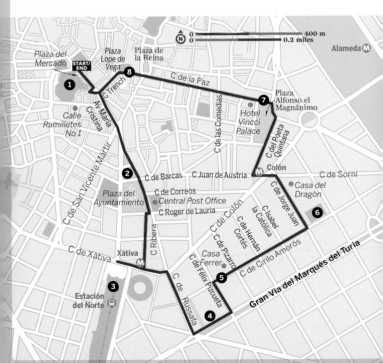

❶ Calle Ramilletes

After sniffing around **Mercado Central** (p54), a Modernista highlight of the city, take in the elaborate stucco facade – with neo-Gothic pilasters above allegories of Valencia's fertility – of **Calle Ramilletes 1**.

❷ Plaza del Ayuntamiento

Follow Avenida María Cristina to **Plaza del Ayuntamiento**, site of the sober **town hall** (p40) and resplendent **central post office**, a lighter neoclassical affair with 1920s flourishes. Drop in and look up to savour its magnificent leaded-glass dome. Valencia's biggest concentration of flower stalls fringes this open square.

❸ Estación del Norte

At the end of Calle Ribera, detour to heart-warming **Estación del Norte** (p39), with its optimistic exterior, cute original Modernista booking area of dark wood, and adjacent hall with elaborate tilework.

❹ Casa Ortega

Take Calle de Russafa, then turn left for **Casa Ortega** at Gran Vía 9, with its ornate floral decoration and balcony supported by a pair of handsome caryatids.

❺ Calle de Cirilo Amorós

Go left along Calle de Félix Pizcueta, then take the first right onto **Calle de Cirilo Amorós**. Lift your gaze above the modern, ground-floor shops to appreciate each building's original structure. Pause by **Casa Ferrer** (No 29), garlanded with stucco roses and ceramic tiling.

❻ Mercado de Colón

Continue northeast to the resplendent **Mercado de Colón** (p87), a chic spot for a drink stop surrounded by Modernista glory. Then head northwest on Calle de Jorge Juan, passing **Casa del Dragón** at No 3, named for its dragon motifs.

❼ Calle de la Paz

Head down Calle del Poeta Quintana and pass the haughty mounted statue of King Jaime I to join **Calle de la Paz**. Back in the 19th century, Hotel Vincci Palace (Palace Hotel) was Valencia's finest. Both it and No 31, opposite, have elaborate, decorated miradors (corner balconies), while No 36 has delicate, leafy iron railings.

❽ Back to the Market

On the corner of Calle de las Comedias, No 21–23 has characteristically magnificent window-and-balcony work and a columned mirador. At the end of Calle de la Paz, continue straight then, at Plaza Lope de Vega, turn left into Calle Trench to return to the Mercado Central.

Sights

Oceanogràfic
AQUARIUM

1 ⊙ MAP P86, B2

Spain's most famous aquarium is the southernmost building of the Ciudad de las Artes y las Ciencias (p80). It's an impressive display, divided into a series of climate zones, reached overground or underground from the central hub building. The sharks, complete with tunnel, are an obvious favourite, while a series of beautiful tanks present species from temperate, Mediterranean, Red Sea and tropical waters. Less happily, the aquarium also keeps captive dolphins and belugas – research suggests this is detrimental to their welfare.

It's not all underwater. An aviary presents wetland birds, while polar regions feature penguins. There are seals, sea lions and walruses, too. Though the dolphin shows are a definite black mark, the aquarium does make a proper effort to present information about climate change and depletion of the marine ecosystem. There's also a 4D cinema. Hours vary by season; check the website for details. (☏ 960 47 06 47; www.oceanografic.org; Camino de las Moreras; adult/child €30.70/22.90, audio guide €3.70, combined ticket with Hemisfèric & Museo de las Ciencias Príncipe Felipe €38.20/28.60; ⊙ 10am-6pm Sun-Fri, to 8pm Sat mid-Sep–mid-Jun, 10am-8pm mid-Jun–mid-Jul & early Sep, 10am-midnight mid-Jul–Aug; 👪)

Mercado de Colón
MARKET

2 ⊙ MAP P86, D2

This magnificent building, now colonised by cafes and boutique food outlets, was formerly a market, built in 1916 to serve the rising bourgeoisie of the new L'Eixample suburb. Its handsome metal skeleton is garnished with Modernista flourishes to create a stunning ensemble. It's a good place to try *horchata* (a sugary drink made from tiger nuts) and a fine refuge for families, as kids can run around and there's food available all day. (☏ 963 37 11 01; www.mercadocolon.es; Calle de Cirilo Amorós; ⊙ 7.30am-2am Sun-Thu, to 3am Fri & Sat)

Museo Fallero
MUSEUM

3 ⊙ MAP P86, A1

At each Fallas festival (p114), just one of the thousands of *ninots*, the figurines that pose at the base of each *falla* (huge statues of papier mâché and polystyrene), is saved from the flames by popular vote. Those reprieved over the years are displayed here. It's fascinating to see their evolution over time, and to see the comical, grotesque, sometimes moving figures up close (☏ 962 08 46 25; www.valencia.es; Plaza Monteolivete 4; adult/child €2/free, Sun free; ⊙ 10am-7pm Mon-Sat, to 2pm Sun)

Eating

Goya

VALENCIAN €€

4 ✕ MAP P86, D4

Decorated with style and featuring real dedication to guests' comfort and pleasure, this busy local classic is outstanding. The menu takes in Valencian favourites such as delicious seafood rices and typical tapas, and includes some more avant-garde foodie bravura. It's all strong on presentation and great on taste. Its blend of traditional values and modern cooking makes it stand out. (☑963 04 18 35; www.goyagalleryrestaurant.com; Calle Burriana 3; mains €13-25; ☺food 1-4pm & 8.15-11.15pm Tue-Sat, 1-4pm Sun)

La Chipirona

SEAFOOD €€

5 ✕ MAP P86, D4

La Chipirona's coolly elegant, pared-back modern decor is attractive, but the warmth of the team here even more so. The menu is principally seafood-focused, and they prepare some very succulent fare in the open kitchen. The crispy house croquettes are a taste sensation, and salmon comes off the robata grill silky and juicy. The set lunch menu is tops for €16.50. (☑640 116024; www.restaurantelachipirona.com; Calle del Maestro Gozalbo 29; mains €12-18; ☺1.30-4pm Tue & Sun, 1.30-4pm & 8.30pm-midnight Wed-Sat)

Sólo del Mar

SEAFOOD €€

6 ✕ MAP P86, A2

A great lunch option when visiting the Ciudad de las Artes y las Ciencias, this innovative place in a residential complex is a fishmonger that doubles as a restaurant and tapas bar at mealtimes. The seafood is of excellent quality, simply and deliciously prepared at very fair prices. (☑963 74 40 45; www.solodelmar.com; Calle Poeta Josep Cervera i Grifol 12, off Avenida Instituto Obrero de Valencia; dishes €7-15; ☺noon-4pm Tue-Thu & Sun, noon-4pm & 8pm-midnight Fri & Sat, open Thu night & closed Sun Jul-Sep)

Las Lunas

FUSION €€

7 ✕ MAP P86, F3

Somewhat tucked away and unassuming, this place has an excellent lunchtime set menu (€12.90 weekdays, €17.90 weekends) that offers brilliant value for creative, succulent cuisine presented with flair and served with a smile. There's always a vegan choice and it does a weekday evening offer, too. (☑695 192336; www.laslunassoulkitchen.com; Calle del Doctor Císcar 39; mains €10-15; ☺1.30-4pm Sun-Tue, 1.30-4pm & 8.30-11pm Wed-Sat; 🛜🍽️)

L'Encís

VALENCIAN €€

8 ✕ MAP P86, C2

Creativity in the kitchen and enthusiastic, committed service characterise this likeable place. The back dining room is a cool,

STA/SHUTTERSTOCK ©

Mercado de Colón (p87)

pleasant spot to enjoy cuisine that borrows from other cultures but uses solid local ingredients. Even such humble cuts as chicken thigh are given quite a makeover; plates are colourful and delicious. The €12.50 weekday lunch special is a steal. (🔊 960 64 45 54; www.facebook.com/lencisvalencia; Calle de Félix Pizcueta 13; mains €11-16; 🕐 1-4pm Tue-Sun & 8.30-11pm Fri & Sat)

Coloniales Huerta TAPAS €€

 9 MAP P86, D3

Occupying a classic centenarian Valencian delicatessen-wine-shop, this dark, welcoming place offers tables among the attractive tiles, bottle shelves and deli counter. Dishes range from the classic – including top-notch charcuterie – to the innovative. There's a worth-

while weekday lunch tapas *menú* (€14.50) and streetside seating. You can drink any wine in the shop for retail price plus a small corkage fee. (🔊 963 34 80 09; www.grupolasucursal.com; Calle del Maestro Gozalbo 13; dishes €12-18; 🕐 restaurant 1.30-4pm & 8.30-11pm or midnight Mon-Sat; 🛜)

Racó del Turia VALENCIAN €€€

 10 MAP P86, E2

Intimate, traditional and upmarket, this classy spot is famous for well-prepared Valencian cuisine. Its rice dishes are famously excellent, particularly its *arroz con bogavante* (rice with lobster). Best to book for weekend lunchtime. (🔊 963 95 15 25; www.racodelturia.com; Calle del Doctor Ciscar 10; mains €16-26; 🕐 1.30-4pm & 8.30-11.30pm)

Abanicos Carbonell (p92)

Casa Vela

DELI €€

11 MAP P86, D2

Uncomplicated and likeable, this longstanding small-goods shop has a bar and squeezes in a couple of tables at mealtimes. Sampler plates of things like *lacón* (pork front leg) are delicious, while heartier fare such as steaks and bean stews are also on hand. Wine is very reasonably priced. (963 51 67 34; www.restaurantecasavela.com; Calle Isabel la Católica 26; dishes €4-16; 10am-4pm & 8pm-midnight Mon-Sat)

La Majada Quesos

CHEESE €€

12 MAP P86, C3

Queso (cheese) connoisseurs will love this bar for its events, tastings and, of course, lots and lots of cheese. Peruse the counter or enter the pungent cheese room that showcases giant wheels of brie and hunks of gouda. Then choose a cava from the wine cellar and pair with a cheese tasting plate that includes locally made specialities. (963 54 50 28; www.lamajadaquesos.com; Calle de Félix Pizcueta 15; cheese plates €17; 11am-midnight Tue-Sat)

Casa Roberto

VALENCIAN €€

13 MAP P86, D4

While there are cheaper rices around, the quality of the ingredients and know-how in the preparation at this well-established restaurant make it a reliable choice. There's a wide selection of options, particularly seafood-based: this is one of the best spots to try rice with lobster

or crayfish. (📞963 95 13 61; http://
casaroberto.es; Calle del Maestro
Gozalbo 19; rice dishes per person
€18-24; ⏱1-4pm & 8.30-11.30pm
Tue-Sat, 1-4pm Sun; 🛜)

Drinking

L'Umbracle Terraza   BAR, CLUB

 14 🚇 MAP P86, B2

At the southern end of the Umbracle walkway within the Ciudad
de las Artes y las Ciencias, this is
a touristy but atmospheric spot
to spend a hot summer night.
After the queue, catch the evening
breeze under the stars on the terrace. The downstairs club **Mya** is
a sweatier experience. Admission
(€12) covers both venues.

You can buy tickets online at
www.pubyfiesta.com. (📞671
668000; www.umbracleterraza.com;
Avenida del Professor López Piñero 5;
⏱midnight-7.30am Thu-Sat)

Mercado de Colón   CAFE

As this visually stunning
Modernista market building
(see **2** ◉ Map p86, D2) devotes itself
mostly to cafes, it's the place for a
bargain breakfast, a leisurely
horchata (cold drink made from
tiger nuts) or an evening mojito.
Just stroll along and take your pick
from the phalanx of places. The
best food is in **Habitual**, downstairs. (www.mercadocolon.es; Calle de
Cirilo Amorós; ⏱7.30am-2am Sun-Thu,
to 3am Fri & Sat; 🛜)

Casa Vela

Sedici BAR

15 MAP P86, E2

This friendly bar fills with a mellow, mixed crowd enjoying its relaxed atmosphere and well-priced *copas* (mixed drinks). It also makes a very acceptable mojito. (☎ 622 015855; www.facebook.com/sedicivalencia16; Calle del Conde de Altea 45; ⏰6pm-2am Mon-Thu, 5pm-3am Fri & Sat; 📶)

Doce Gin Club COCKTAIL BAR

16 MAP P86, D3

This fun bar takes gin seriously. Doce Gin Club made the Guinness World Records in 2015 with 450 gin varieties; though it's since lost the record, it now claims to have more than 500 types. Connoisseurs can try everything from locally made gins to rare editions of Bombay Sapphire and Beefeater, all expertly prepared. Tapas and other cocktails also available. (☎ 963 81 52 12; Calle del Almirante Cadarso 12; ⏰5pm-2.30am)

Entertainment

Palau de les Arts Reina Sofía OPERA

17 MAP P86, A1

This spectacular arts venue, part of the Ciudad de las Artes y las Ciencias, offers mostly opera, but also concerts and recitals. (box office ☎ 902 20 23 83; www.lesarts.com; Avenida del Professor López Piñero 1)

Shopping

Abanicos Carbonell ARTS & CRAFTS

18 MAP P86, B4

This historic fan-maker, in business since 1810, offers hand-painted manual cooling units ranging from a very reasonable €10 for the basic but pretty ones, to works by famous fan painters that run to thousands of euros. It's been run by the same family for five generations. (☎ 963 41 53 95; www.abanicoscarbonell.com; Calle de Castellón 21; ⏰9.30am-1.30pm & 4-8pm Mon-Fri)

Linda Vuela a Rio COSMETICS

19 MAP P86, C3

A very elegant perfume shop specialising in boutique scents sourced from around the

A Classic on the Avenue

Something of a legendary local stop for a morning coffee or a pre-lunch beer or vermouth, **Aquarium** (Map p86, E2; ☎ 963 51 00 40; Gran Vía del Marqués del Turia 57; ⏰7am-1am Mon-Fri, 8am-1.30am Sat & Sun; 📶) is an old-fashioned place with a lived-in interior, wood panelling and white-coated waiters. Outdoor seating puts you in the buzz of the traffic but also by the flow of people. Indoors lets you scope out the cognac-and-cigar-gnarled local characters.

world. It's an enjoyably different experience, set apart from the supermodel-driven brands. The entrance on a corner of the elegant avenue is marked only by monkeys accompanying Rio de Janeiro's Corcovado statue of Christ. (📞963 51 77 46; http://linda-vuelaario.com; Gran Vía del Marqués del Turia 31; ⏰10am-2pm & 5-8.30pm Mon-Sat)

Place
CLOTHING

20 🔒 MAP P86, C3

With several stallholders in one communal space, Place offers a bit of everything, from unique small-designer pieces to vintage clothing and creative accessories. (📞963 94 11 02; http://placevalencia.com; Calle de Cirilo Amorós 24; ⏰10am-2.30pm & 5-9pm Mon-Fri, from 10.30am Sat)

Trufas Martínez
FOOD

21 🔒 MAP P86, B3

The aromas are mouthwatering in this unassuming shop, where 80 years of experience have resulted in chocolate truffle perfection, as well as succulent marrons glacés and rich, dark handmade chocolates. The packaging is almost as elegant as the treasures within. (📞963 51 62 89; www.trufasmartinez.com; Calle de Russafa 12; ⏰9.30am-8.30pm Mon-Sat year-round, 10am-2pm Sun Oct-Jun)

Courtside Action

Valencia's basketball team, **Valencia Basket Club** (📞963 95 70 84; www.valenciabasket.com; Avenida Hermanos Maristas), has had a pretty good time of it in the top division (Liga ACB), winning the league in 2017, though, as in football, the title normally gets won by Real Madrid or Barcelona. The season runs from October to May. You can buy tickets online or at several sales points around the city.

Manglano
FOOD & DRINKS

22 🔒 MAP P86, D2

Downstairs in the Mercado de Colón (p87), Manglano offers a selection of brilliant cheeses, quality charcuterie and some wine. (📞963 52 88 54; www.facebook.com/charcuteriasmanglano; ⏰9am-9pm Mon-Sat)

Tenda Granota
SPORTS & OUTDOORS

23 🔒 MAP P86, D1

It's sometimes easy to forget that Valencia has two football teams, so head here to pick up a Barcelona-like replica shirt of perennial football underdogs Levante. The shop's size, compared to Valencia's megastore (p45), emphasises the status gap between the teams. (📞902 220 304; http://tienda.levanteud.com; Plaza de los Pinazos 6; ⏰10am-9pm Mon-Sat)

Explore ✪
Russafa

The new town's most captivating corner, the district of Russafa (Spanish: Ruzafa) may be comparatively compact but it packs a weighty punch. A downmarket barrio (neighbourhood) turned trendy, by day its collection of quirky galleries and vintage shops keep people entertained, while by night it offers the city's best eating and cafe-bar nightlife, a buzzing hub of quality tapas, modish vermouth bars, literary cafes and innovative cultural offerings. It's a district with its own very distinctive feel and an essential Valencian evening experience, particularly at weekends.

The Short List

o **Dining (p99)** *Hitting one of the multitude of quality restaurants and tapas joints, such as Canalla Bistro or El Rodamón de Russafa.*

o **Cafe Culture (p96)** *Looking the part by thumbing through a novel or chatting to locals in a language exchange at places such as Cafe Berlin.*

o **Vintage Shopping (p104)** *Searching for retro rags at one of Valencia's best vintage-clothing shops, Madame Mim.*

o **Nightlife (p96)** *Pounding the dance floor at clubs such as Piccadilly and Xtra Lrge.*

Getting There & Around

🚌 Several buses pass through Russafa, including the 35 from the Ciudad de las Artes y las Ciencias, the 6 and the 7.

Ⓜ The closest stations are Xàtiva and Bailén.

🚶 Russafa is in easy walking distance of the southern part of the old town.

Russafa Map on p98

Ubik Café (p102) CUM OKOLO/ALAMY ©

A Night Out in Russafa

Russafa is Valencia's best place for an evening meal, with a staggering variety of options in a small area. Most lean towards modern, fusion cuisine, vegetarian or international specialities. It gets very busy at weekends, when the buzz is intoxicating. Tapas portions mean that you can go from bar to bar, trying different creations. It's the centrepiece of a great night out.

Start Cafe Berlin
Finish Piccadilly Downtown Club
Length 2km; time depends on you

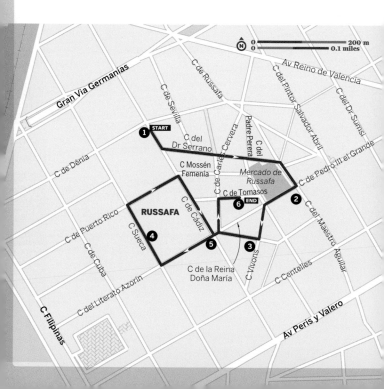

❶ Boho Beginnings

Start off the evening at **Cafe Berlin** (📞 640 781372; www.facebook.com/cafeberlinvalencia; Calle de Cádiz 22; 🕐6pm-1am Mon-Wed, 6pm-2.30am Thu & Fri, 4.30pm-2.30am Sat, 4.30pm-1am Sun; 🛜). Russafa does bohemian so well, and this is one of many quality cafe-bars of this type, offering a lounge-like ambience with books, art exhibitions and decent drinks, including well-made cocktails. There's loads of atmosphere. They do language-exchange sessions, a good way to meet locals.

❷ Modern Tapas

The eclectic range of tapas is delicious at **La Tasqueta del Mercat** (📞 633 285155; www.facebook.com/latasquetadelmercat; Calle del Maestro Aguilar 2; tapas €3-10; 🕐1.30-3.45pm & 8.30-11pm Tue-Thu, 1.30-4pm & 8.30pm-midnight Fri & Sat; 🛜), a bustling modern eatery near the market. Options are available à la carte or through a series of sampler menus (€15 to €22). We particularly like the aubergines in soy sauce.

❸ Pizza & Beer

Likeably unrefined, the bustle extends out onto the street at **La Finestra** (📞 963 81 89 85; www.facebook.com/lafinestrapizzacafe; Calle Vivons 16; mini-pizzas €1.50; 🕐noon-1am; 🛜), a popular backstreet eatery. The principal drawcards are their delicious mini-pizzas, for which staff choose the toppings for you. Beer is cheap too, so plan ahead to make sure it's your round.

❹ Around the World

The deal at excellent **El Rodamón de Russafa** (📞963 21 80 14; www.elrodamon.com; Calle Sueca 47; tapas €7-13; 🕐2-4pm & 8.30-11.30pm Wed-Mon, evenings only Jul–mid-Sep; 🛜) is that they've picked their favourite dishes encountered around the world and made a Valencian tapas plate out of them, so you can pick from tacos, curry, tartare, tataki and numerous other eclectic dishes. It's modern and buzzy, with excellent staff, great wines and high quality throughout.

❺ Backstage Pass

Though it's been dolled up a bit since the old days, the **Backstage** (📞963 34 89 13; Calle del Literato Azorín 1; 🕐4pm-1.30am Sun-Thu, to 2am Fri & Sat) bar on a key Russafa intersection is still a classic reference point. It's small, intimate and characterful: a great place for a post-dinner drink. True to its name, it preserves a bit of after-show ambience with light-bulb mirrors and glory-days posters.

❻ Dance the Night Away

To round off the night, it's lots of fun at the sizeable **Piccadilly Downtown Club** (Calle de Tomasos 12; 🕐1am-7.30am Fri & Sat nights; 🛜). Music focuses on major hits from the '80s and '90s, so there's no excuse not to dance. There's also a silent room, where you don headphones and choose from different sounds. Cover (€10 to €15) includes one or two drinks; prebook online at www.xceed.me.

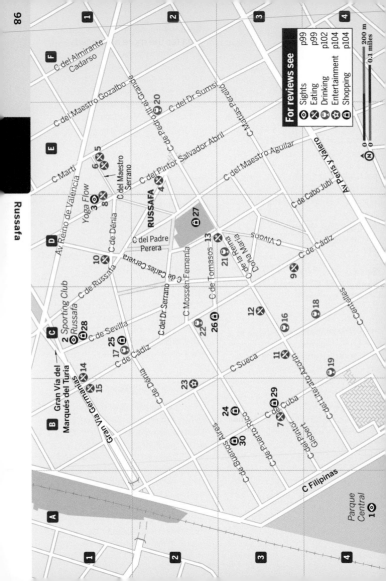

Russafa

F
C del Almirante Cadarso

C del Maestro Gozalbo

C del Maestro Serrano

C Martí

Yoga Flow 3 🟢
8 🟢

E
6 🟢 5
4 🟢

C del Pintor Salvador Abril

C de Pedro III el Grande

20 🟢

C del Dr Sumsi

C Mateu Pestor

RUSSAFA

C del Maestro Aguilar

C de Cabo Jubí

Av Peris y Valero

D
Av Reino de Valencia

C de Dénia

10 🟢

C del Padre Perera

C de Carles Cervera

C Mossén Femenía

13 🟢
21 🟢

C de la Reina

C Doña María

C Vivons

C de Cádiz

27 🟢

9 🟢

C
Sporting Club 2 🟢
Russafa
28 🟢

C de Sevilla

C de Russafa

C del Dr Serrano

C de Tomasos

25 🟢
17 🟢

C de Cádiz

26 🟢
22 🟢

12 🟢

16 🟢

18 🟢

C Sueca

11 🟢

19 🟢

C de Castellar

B
Gran Vía del Marqués del Turia

14 🟢
15 🟢

Gran Vía Germanías

C de Dénia

23 🟢

C de Buenos Aires

C de Puerto Rico

24 🟢

C de Cuba

7 🟢 29 🟢

C del Pintor Gisbert

C del Literato Azorín

30 🟢

A
Parque Central
1 🟢

C Filipinas

For reviews see
🟢 Sights	p99
🟢 Eating	p99
🟢 Drinking	p102
🟢 Entertainment	p104
🟢 Shopping	p104

0 ——— 200 m
0 ——— 0.1 miles

N

Sights

Parque Central
PARK

1 ◎ MAP P98, A4

A long time in the works, this park is the first stage of what is conceived as a civic space to join the two halves of Valencia that are still separated by the train line, which will eventually be put underground. It's a pretty, romantic, formal park with palms, paths to stroll and heritage railway buildings to admire, as well as plenty of spots for kids to play. (📞963 51 08 88; www.valenciaparquecentral.es; Calle Filipinas; ⏰8am-7pm Nov-Feb, to 9pm Mar-Oct)

Sporting Club Russafa
GALLERY

2 ◎ MAP P98, C1

Once the HQ of the local football club, this offbeat gallery space is run by a cooperative not-for-profit arts organisation. Its exhibitions are often worth a look, and it hosts arts-related workshops, performances, talks and other events. (www.sportingclubrussafa.com; Calle de Sevilla 5; admission free; ⏰exhibitions often 5.30-8.30pm Mon-Sat)

Yoga Flow
YOGA

3 ◎ MAP P98, D1

This modern yoga studio offers yoga and meditation classes in English and Spanish in two fresh and bright studios. You'll find everything from hatha flow

sessions for beginners to aerial yoga for the more advanced. Prices drop for more than one class. (📞603 682253; www.yoga flowvlc.com; Calle del Pintor Salvador Abril 9; classes €16; ⏰Mon-Fri)

Eating

Dos Estaciones
SPANISH €€€

4 ✗ MAP P98, E2

Two talented chefs oversee this small restaurant, where an open kitchen and welcoming folk provide a personal gourmet experience. Some extraordinary creations are produced here at a very reasonable price; freshness and innovation are guaranteed, and they'll easily tailor things to your dietary needs and mood. There's also pleasant outdoor seating. One of Russafa's best choices. (📞963 03 46 70; www.restaurante2estaciones.com; Calle del Pintor Salvador Abril 28; mains €19-23, degustation menus €35-50; ⏰1.30-3.45pm Tue & Thu-Sat, 8.30-11pm Tue-Sat)

Cervecería Maipi
TAPAS €€

5 ✗ MAP P98, E1

Far more traditional than most of trendy Russafa, this small tapas bar is a real delight. Delicious no frills dishes use fresh market ingredients of excellent quality and the prices, though not marked, are more than fair. (📞963 73 57 09; www.facebook.com/maipi.bar; Calle del Maestro José Serrano 1; dishes €5-16; ⏰1.30-4pm & 8.30-11pm Tue-Sat)

Canalla Bistro

FUSION €€

6 MAP P98, E1

Chic but commodious, with an interior featuring packing crates, cartoon chickens and other decorative quirks, this is where top Valencian chef Ricard Camarena (p115) can be a little more light-hearted. Sensationally presented dishes draw their inspiration from street food from around the world. Creative, fun and delicious. (☏963 74 05 09; www.canallabistro.com; Calle del Maestro José Serrano 5; mains €10-17; ☉1.30-3.30pm & 8-11pm; 🛜)

Dulce de Leche

CAFF €

7 MAP P98, B3

Delicious sweet and savoury snacks with an Argentine twist are the stock-in-trade of this delicately decorated corner cafe. The coffee is organic, the juices hit the spot and the service is quality. It looks posh but prices are reasonable. Weekend brunch is well priced and tasty, but you might have to bring out your Mr Hyde to bag a street table. (☏963 03 59 49; www.facebook.com/DulceDeLecheRuzafa; Calle del Pintor Gisbert 2; brunch €8; ☉9am-9pm; 🛜)

Mood Food

FUSION €€

8 MAP P98, D1

The harmonious interior of this feel-good place is the scene for an exquisite line in tapas and small plates, blending Spanish and Japanese influences to fine effect, with some touches from elsewhere around the world. The weekday

set menu is fine value for €15. Service is amiable. Best to book. (☏961 05 02 69; www.facebook.com/moodfoodrestaurant; Calle del Pintor Salvador Abril 7; mains €16-19; ☉2-4pm & 8-11pm Tue-Sat; 🛜)

Casa Viva

VEGAN €

9 MAP P98, D3

The Valencia branch of a rural restaurant makes an enticing stop for its effusively cordial welcome and inventive, colourful vegetarian and vegan dishes presented with élan. Decor is cute, with low seats and plenty of greenery. (☏963 03 47 13; Calle de Cádiz 76; mains €6-13; ☉1-3.45pm & 8.30-11pm Wed-Mon; 🖊)

Buñolería El Contraste

CAFE €

10 MAP P98, D1

Valencians have been coming to this corner cafe since the end of the 19th century to enjoy *buñuelos*. Made with pumpkin, this traditional Valencian snack is similar to a doughnut and particularly popular during the Fallas festival in March. Grab a bagful of deep-fried golden goodness and dip in sugar or hot chocolate for the sweetest of treats. (☏963 73 46 11; www.elcontraste.com; Calle San Valero 12; buñuelos €0.60; ☉8.15am-8.30pm Mon-Fri)

La Cooperativa del Mar

SEAFOOD €

11 MAP P98, C3

This former fish shop has been done up beautifully into a bright and atmospheric bar that specialises in colourful tins of fish and seafood – quality stuff, most of it Portuguese in origin. Try some *mejillones en escabeche* (pickled mussels), an ideal aperitif with a vermouth or a seawater-flavoured craft beer. (📞963 22 44 42; www. lacooperativadelmar.com; Calle del Literato Azorín 18; tapas €3-6; ⏱7pm-midnight Mon-Thu, to 1am Fri, 12.30-4pm & 7pm-1am Sat & Sun; 🛜)

Copenhagen   VEGETARIAN €

 12 🍴 MAP P98, C3

Bright and vibrant, the buzz from this popular vegetarian restaurant seems to spread a contagion of good cheer all along the street. It does a very toothsome soy burger as well as top homemade pasta, but it's all pretty tasty. (📞963 28 99 28; www.grupocopenhagen.com;

Calle del Literato Azorín 8; dishes €9-11; ⏱1.30-4pm & 8.30-11.30pm Thu-Mon, 1.30-4pm Tue & Wed; 🛜🖊)

Osteria Vino e Cucina   ITALIAN €

13 🍴 MAP P98, D3

This tiny restaurant serves authentic Italian food with a smile. The handwritten menu offers dishes made with ingredients sourced from Russafa market across the road, and the open kitchen serves perfect al dente pasta. Make the charming waitress' day by ordering one of her homemade desserts. A sister restaurant, at Calle de Pedro III el Grande, is a five-minute walk away. (📞962 06 61 72; www. facebook.com/osteriavinoecucina; Calle de Tomasos 20; pastas €8-10, mains €8-12; ⏱1.30-4pm & 8.30-11pm Sun-Thu, to 11.30pm Fri & Sat)

Mercado de Russafa (p105)

Ultramarinos Agustín Rico

DELI €

14 🍴 MAP P98, C1

On a busy corner, this spacious, brightly lit deli and bar is decorated with legs of *jamón* (ham) and shelves of wine. Perch at the bar to enjoy, or order a *bocadillo* to take away and watch the owner stuff half a baguette with freshly sliced *jamón serrano* and cheese, drizzled with olive oil. (📞 963 41 47 71; www. facebook.com/ultramarinosagustinrico; cnr Gran Via Germanías & Calle de Cádiz; bocadillos €4-6; ⏰ 9am-3.30pm & 6pm-1.30am Mon-Sat)

Mercado San Valero

FOOD HALL €

15 🍴 MAP P98, B1

The city's first indoor street-food market has a bar and 10 food stands serving everything from poke bowls and oysters to burgers and beers, including stalls specialising in avocados and beef. You'll find a snack to suit every taste – but prices are on the high side. Gets busy on weekends. (http://mercadosanvalero.com; Gran Via Germanías 21; burgers €8-9.50; ⏰ noon-midnight Mon-Thu, to 1am Fri, 11am-1pm Sat, 11am-midnight Sun)

Drinking

Ubik Café

BAR, CAFE

16 🍺 MAP P98, C3

This child-friendly cafe, bar and bookshop is a comfy place to lounge and browse. It has a short, well-selected list of wines and serves cheese and cold-meat platters, salads and plenty of Italian specialities. *'Como en casa',* as they say in Spanish, meaning it's welcoming and homey. It offers language-exchange sessions, too. (📞 963 74 12 55; http://ubikcafe. blogspot.com; Calle del Literato Azorín 13; ⏰ 5pm-midnight Mon & Tue, noon-12.30am Wed, Thu & Sun, noon-2am Fri & Sat; 📶 👫)

Slaughterhouse

BAR

17 🍺 MAP P98, C1

Once a butcher's shop (hence its name, also inspired by the similarly titled Kurt Vonnegut novel), Slaughterhouse abounds in books – new, old, for sale and simply for browsing. There's a limited menu of burgers, salads and cheeses, with every dish (€7 to €10) having a 1970s literary or pop-culture reference. (📞 960 22 38 20; www.facebook. com/slaughterhousefoodbooks; Calle de Dénia 22; ⏰ 7pm-midnight; 📶)

Planet Valencia

LESBIAN

18 🍺 MAP P98, C4

Right in the thick of things in Russafa, this bar is the perfect after-tapas destination at weekends for girls looking for girls, but it's a fun place for anyone. (📞 963 22 03 06; www. facebook.com/PlanetValencia; Calle Sueca 63; ⏰ 11pm-3.30am Thu-Sat; 📶)

La Boba y el Gato Rancio

GAY

19 🍺 MAP P98, C4

Run by genuinely welcoming folk, this relaxed gay cafe-bar is lined with elegant portraits of pretty boys. They mix a great cocktail and the small outdoor terrace is a sociable spot. A top spot for a casual drink. (962 06 63 54; www.facebook.com/labobayelgatorancio; Calle de Cuba 59; ⏰7pm-1am Sun-Thu, 7pm-2.30am Fri & Sat; 📶)

Jardín Urbano
CAFE

20 🚇 MAP P98, E2

Charmingly eclectic, the interior of this inviting corner cafe features books, a fountain, plants and artworks. Slightly removed from the hectic central Russafa scene, this is a spot for a quiet drink with friends or a read of a novel at one of the outdoor tables. It's all vegan, with various nondairy milks available, and it does tapas. (961 13 32 07; www.facebook.com/jardinurbanoruzafa; Calle de Pedro III El Grande 26; ⏰10am-12.30am Sun-Thu, to 1.30am Fri & Sat; 📶)

Cuatro Monos
BAR

21 🚇 MAP P98, D3

A cosily bohemian Italian-run bar with a welcoming vibe, Cuatro Monos attracts regulars and travellers alike. The bar mixes monkey-inspired art and soft toys with sofas, high bar tables and pavement seating. The friendly staff can recommend a custom cocktail (Purple Monkey, anyone?) or pour a refreshing on-tap international beer or local IPA. (Four Monkeys; 601 079146; www.facebook.com/cuatromonosvalencia; Calle de la Reina

> ### Drinking the Local Water
>
> *Agua de Valencia* is a popular local drink and refreshing indeed, but it couldn't be further from water. The usual recipe is to mix cava, orange juice and a healthy dash of gin and/or vodka. It goes down a treat on a summer's day but packs a punch.

Doña María 7; ⏰4pm-1.30am Mon-Fri, from 3pm Sat & Sun)

Xtra Lrge
CLUB

Spread over 600 sq metres, this underground club (see 15 ✕ Map p98, B1) merits its outsized name. All soft pastel colours on brute metal and concrete, it offers live DJs across three spaces. There's no cover charge and a pretty relaxed atmosphere. The crowd is more 30-somethings than youngsters. (654 114435; www.facebook.com/xlxtralrge; Gran Via Germanías 21; ⏰midnight-3.30am Fri & Sat)

Café Tocado
BAR

22 🚇 MAP P98, C2

With the rich reds and romance of a French belle époque locale, this place backs it up by actually having a small cabaret theatre alongside the intimate main bar. The location on a central Russafa corner is tops though service can be gruff. (Calle de Cádiz 44; ⏰7pm-3am Tue-Sat; 📶)

PENNY KIDD/LONELY PLANET ©

Gnomo

Entertainment

Café Mercedes Jazz   LIVE MUSIC

23 ⭐ MAP P98, B2

This super jazz club is run by a real aficionado and has quality acoustics. There's live music weekly (cover €10) as well as DJs. A fine after-dinner hideaway. (📞960 62 04 42; www.cafemercedes.es; Calle Sueca 27; 🕐8pm-1.30am Thu, to 3.30am Fri & Sat, 6-11.30pm Sun)

Shopping

Madame Mim   VINTAGE

24 🔒 MAP P98, B3

Many Valencians would say this is the city's best vintage shop, and we're always intrigued by what it has in stock. As well as clothes,

there's a quirky line of interesting objects that's definitely worth a peek. (📞963 25 59 41; www.facebook.com/madame.mim.shop; Calle de Puerto Rico 30; 🕐11am-2.30pm & 5.30-9.30pm Tue, Thu & Fri, 11am-2.30pm & 6-10pm Sat)

Kowalski Bellas Artes   ART

25 🔒 MAP P98, C1

This romantic treasure trove of a shop celebrates art – indeed the owner is an artist and is often drawing or painting in the shop. Paints, books, vinyls, leather boots and more; it's a beautiful and curious place to browse. (📞963 12 52 22; www.facebook.com/kowalskibellas artes; Calle de Dénia 20; 🕐10am-2pm & 5-9pm Mon-Fri, 10.30am-2.30pm & 6-9pm Sat, closed Sat Jul & Aug)

Librería Bartleby COMICS, BOOKS

26 MAP P98, C2

Bright and cheerful, Bartleby specialises in comics, but also has an interesting selection of other books. It sells wine too, and you can sip a glass of something while you're browsing. (963 23 71 84; www.facebook.com/libreriabartleby; Calle de Cádiz 50; 10am-2pm & 5-10pm Mon-Sat)

Mercado de Russafa MARKET

27 MAP P98, D2

Forget Valencia's glorious Modernista markets for now. This concrete brutalist monster plunked in the middle of Russafa, cheered up by brightly painted louvred friezes, is where it's at for good, fresh produce in this *barrio*. Well worth a browse. (963 74 40 25; http://mercatderussafa.com; Calle de la Reina Doña María; 7am-3pm Mon-Sat)

Paranoid CLOTHING

28 MAP P98, C1

Design your own T-shirt in this excellent shop, which also has preprinted tees to choose from. Its offbeat sideline is retro musical instruments, and making its own weird electronic instruments from old bits and pieces. If you're lucky (depending on your tastes) you may catch a concert. (960 07 07 42; www.paranoidtees.net; Calle de Sevilla 7; 11am-2pm & 5-9pm Mon-Fri)

D Tes TEA

29 MAP P98, B3

A range of really beautiful teapots and an intriguing selection of teas and other infusions are this atmospheric shop's stock in trade. The aromas alone make it worth a visit. (680 445380; www.facebook.com/dtesmagatzem; Calle de Cuba 43; 10.30am-2pm & 6-9pm Mon-Sat)

Gnomo GIFTS & SOUVENIRS

30 MAP P98, B3

An original Russafa shop displaying a wide range of contemporarily styled designer objects. It's the perfect place to pick up an unusual gift for somebody at home. (963 73 72 67; www.gnomo.eu; Calle de Cuba 32; 11am-2pm & 5-9pm Mon-Sat)

Explore ◈

Northern & Eastern Valencia

This large swath of the city beyond the Turia riverbed park includes the two principal universities, so it's well stocked with bars, restaurants and nightclubs. The Turia itself, a 9km ribbon of park, is a strollable highlight. The main city art gallery and Valencia football team are pillars of local culture, while the suburb of Benimaclet is lively with alternative, community-driven happenings.

The Short List

∘ **Jardines del Turia (p113)** Congratulating planners who converted the riverbed into a glorious park and not a six-lane bypass.

∘ **Museo de Bellas Artes (p108)** Contemplating golden-age masters and local lad Joaquín Sorolla.

∘ **Valencia Club de Fútbol (p118)** Revelling in the atmosphere as the team tries to impress the nation's most demanding fans.

∘ **Benimaclet (p110)** Taking in the countercultural vibe of this traditional workers' barrio (neighbourhood).

∘ **Nightlife (p118)** Showing the night no mercy in legendary venues such as Black Note.

Getting There & Around

🚌 Numerous bus lines cross the area and are the best option for reaching many places.

Ⓜ Aragón is handy for the Valencia stadium, and Pont de Fusta is close to the Museo de Bellas Artes. For Plaza Xúquer, head to Aragón, Amistat or Universitat Politécnica. Benimaclet has its own stop and is also close to Vincente Zaragozá.

Northern & Eastern Valencia Map on p112

Museo de Bellas Artes (p108) RRRAINBOW/SHUTTERSTOCK ©

Top Experience 📸
See Art in a Former Seminary at Museo de Bellas Artes

Valencia's main art gallery is a somewhat understated spot across the dry riverbed from the old town. Housed in part of a former seminary, it boasts a rather impressive collection of local artists and Spanish masters. Bright and spacious, this gallery ranks among Spain's best.

◎ MAP P112, B2

San Pío V

📞 963 87 03 00

www.museobellasartes valencia.gva.es

Calle de San Pío V 9

admission free

🕙 10am-8pm Tue-Sun

Joaquín Sorolla

A dedicated wing is devoted to this versatile Valencian artist (1863-1923), whose work ranges from the openly Francophile to idealised country scenes to intimate family portraits. *María convaleciente* is a stunning depiction of his daughter, whose look seems to sum up illness as well as the doubts of a young woman entering adulthood. Sorolla at his best seems capable of capturing the whole spirit of an era through sensitive portraiture. The galleries also feature his contemporaries and those he influenced.

Francisco Goya

A handful of paintings against shadowy background by Spain's master of darkness are a high point of the upper floor. Though some may seem standard portraits, Goya's mastery of the unquiet behind the subjects' eyes marks him out as a painterly force to be reckoned with. Even the kids playing seem haunted by some impending doom.

Diego Velázquez

Vying with Goya and Picasso for the title of Spain's greatest painter, Diego Velázquez took Spanish art to the heights of its 'golden age' in the 17th century. His powerful *Autorretrato* (self-portrait) here is one of his masterworks. Look out, too, for his depiction of the dead Beato Simón de Rojas.

The Ribaltas

Francisco Ribalta and his son Juan were important painters in Valencia in the late 16th and early 17th centuries and are reasonably well represented here. Juan's *Preparativos para la crucifixión* is beautifully composed, and his father's evolution from mannerism to a more naturalistic style is visible.

★ **Top Tips**

○ It's free, it's close to the old town, it's open until 8pm and it doesn't close for lunch, so this is one of your more flexible options when planning your sightseeing agenda.

○ Don't miss a stroll in the adjacent Jardines del Real (p113) while you're in this part of town.

✕ **Take a Break**

The gallery has a pleasant indoor-outdoor cafe space that does decent lunches.

Fancy continuing with the artistic theme? Try dining at nearby Lienzo (p64); its name means 'canvas', and the food certainly is an art form.

Northern & Eastern Valencia Museo de Bellas Artes

Walking Tour 🚶

A Cultural Evening in Benimaclet

Once a separate community in the Valencian farmlands, Benimaclet, a short stroll, tram or metro ride from the centre, conserves a village feel. Its network of bars and cafes are anything but provincial, however. Cool, arty, socially aware and innovative, they produce a constant array of cultural events that mean there's something going on here every night of the week.

Start Centro Instructivo Musical; Metro Benimaclet

Finish La Gramola

Length 2km; one hour

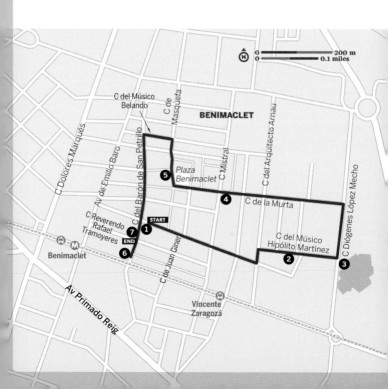

❶ Cultural Hub

The **Centro Instructivo Musical** (📞963 69 18 79; www.cimbenimaclet.com; Calle del Barón de San Petrillo 14; 🕓8am-midnight Mon-Fri plus weekend events) in the heart of the *barrio* doesn't look much with its big bare interior, but in many ways it's the soul of the community and a driving force for the cultural projects in the area. Exhibitions, classes, concerts or just a beer and a game of pool: drop by and see what's on.

❷ Pizza Break

Cosy and convivial, with Tibetan prayer flags fluttering, **L'Olegari** (📞960 62 37 87; www.facebook.com/olegaribenimaclet; Calle del Músico Hipólito Martínez 8; tapas €1.50-5; 🕓11am-1am; 🛜📶) makes a great snack break, serving up delicious little pizzas. Order the number you want and they'll decide on the toppings (dietary requests catered for).

❸ An Unusual Building

An astonishing sight, the '80s architectural project **Espai Vert** (Calle Diógenes López Mecho) looks like the mother ship has landed on the edge of Benimaclet. A riot of unusual angles, protruding green spaces and quirky shapes, it was built as a cooperative aimed at developing a different way of communal living. The spacious apartments all have a garden, whatever the level.

❹ La Murta

Bohemian even by Benimaclet standards, this all-day **cafe, bar and tapas stop** (📞961 33 69 71; www.facebook.com/barlamurta; Calle de la Murta 14; tapas €4-6; 🕓7.30am-midnight Mon-Thu, to 1.30am Fri, 9am-1.30am Sat, to 11.30pm Sun; 🛜📶) is a politically active place that's simple, cheap and informal. The list of tapas on the wall has out-of-the-ordinary offerings. Most are good, some are very good. Vegetarian options include melt-in-the-mouth crumbed goat's cheese and croquettes.

❺ The Plaza

The peaceful little plaza breaks up the grid-like street plan. The grungy rock bar **Glop** (📞633 014043; Plaza Benimaclet 3; 🕓6pm-3.30am Mon-Sat, from 8.30pm Sun; 🛜) hasn't changed for years. It doesn't take itself too seriously and the good-natured crowd spills onto the square on summer evenings.

❻ Dinner and Drinks

If you want a fuller meal to round out your visit, **Pata Negra** (📞963 89 09 54; www.facebook.com/patabenimaclet; Calle del Barón de San Petrillo 3; tapas €6-12, mains €14-19; 🕓2-5pm & 9pm-midnight Mon-Sat) is an attractive, romantic place to dine with offbeat items giving it the feel of a curiosity shop.

❼ La Gramola

Just up the road, **La Gramola** (📞660 829084; Calle del Barón de San Petrillo 9; 🕓6pm-2am Mon-Sat, to 1am Sun; 🛜) does a great mojito. The bar is lined with old vinyl; the music selection has jazz as its backbone.

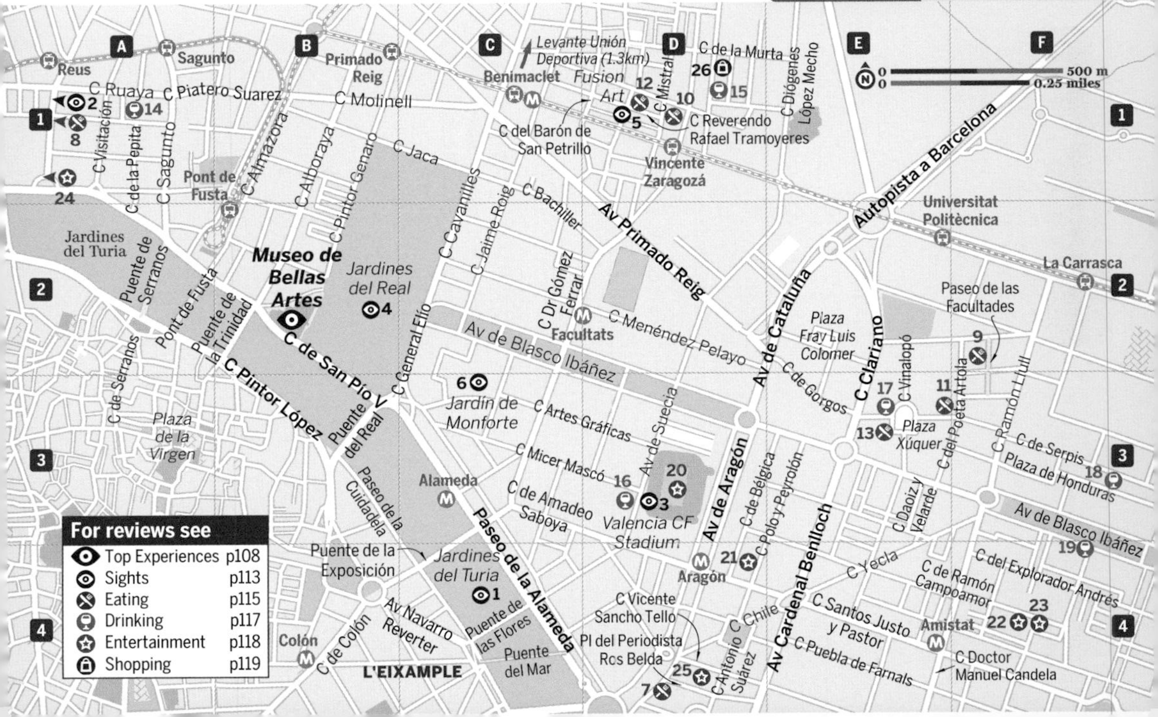

Northern & Eastern Valencia

500 m
0.25 miles

A **B** **C** **D** **E** **F**

L'EIXAMPLE

Museo de Bellas Artes

Universitat Politècnica

C del Explorador Andrés

C Doctor Manuel Candela

For reviews see	
Top Experiences	p108
Sights	p113
Eating	p115
Drinking	p117
Entertainment	p118
Shopping	p119

Streets and labels visible on map:

Reus, Saguntò, C Ruaya, C Platero Suárez, C Visitación, C de la Pepita, Pont de Fusta, Jardines del Turia, C de la Murta, Diógenes López Mecho, C Reverendo Rafael Tramoyeres, C Mistral, Vincente Zaragozá, Art, Fusión, Levante Unión Deportiva (1.3km), Primado Reig, C Molinell, C Pintor Genaro, Jardines del Real, C Cavanilles, C Jaca, C Bachiller, C del Barón de San Petrillo, Av Primado Reig, C Menéndez Pelayo, C Dr Gómez Ferrer, Facultats, La Carrasca, C de Serpis, Plaza de Honduras, Av de Blasco Ibáñez, Paseo de las Facultades, C del Poeta Artola, C Ramón Lull, C Ciriano, Plaza Fray Luis Colomer, C de Gorgos, Vinalopó, Plaza Xúquer, C Daoíz y Velarde, C Santos Justo y Pastor, C del Ramón Campoamor, Amistat, C de Puebla de Farnals, Av Cardenal Benlloch, C de Bélgica, C de Polo y Peyrolón, Av de Aragón, C Chile, C Antonio Suárez, Av de Suecia, Valencia CF Stadium, C de Amadeo Saboya, C Micer Mascó, C de Artes Gráficas, C Vicente Sancho Tello, Pl del Periodista Ros Belda, Aragón, Av de Blasco Ibáñez, Jardín de Monforte, C General Elío, Puente del Real, C de San Pío V, Paseo de la Alameda, Jardines del Turia, Alameda, Paseo de la Cuidadela, Puente de la Exposición, Av Navarro Reverter, Puente de las Flores, Puente del Mar, C de Colón, Colón, Puente de Fusta, C Sagunto, C Pintor López, C de la Trinidad, Puente de la Trinidad, Plaza de la Virgen, C de Serranos, Puente de Serranos, Jardines del Turia, Aljorraya, C Almazora, Alborayá

Autopista a Barcelona

Sights

Jardines del Turia   PARK

1 MAP P112, C4

Stretching the length of Río Turia's former course, this 9km-long lung of green is a fabulous mix of playing fields, lawns, playgrounds, and cycling, jogging and walking paths. As it curves around the eastern part of the city, it's also a pleasant way of getting around. See Lilliputian kids scrambling over a magnificent, ever-patient Gulliver, south of the Palau de la Música concert hall. Check out the walking tour on p138. (🚶)

Bombas Gens   GALLERY

2 ◉ MAP P112, A1

This conversion of a handsome art-deco factory that once made hydraulic pumps has created an intriguing space for modern art. There's a particularly good photography collection, displayed to great advantage in the high-ceilinged spaces. The project, which receives no public funding, also has a cafeteria for underprivileged youths and holds the restaurant (p115) of local master chef Ricard Camarena. (📞963 46 38 56; www.bombasgens.com; Avenida de Burjassot 54; admission free; ⏰5-9pm Wed, 11am-2pm & 5-9pm Thu-Sun)

Valencia CF Stadium   STADIUM

3 ◉ MAP P112, D3

The guided visit to Valencia's famous Mestalla stadium takes you

Valencia CF Stadium

to the press room, the changing rooms and out onto the hallowed turf. Hours change by season and according to fixtures, so check the website in advance. (Mestalla; 📞963 37 26 26; www.valenciacf.com; Avenida de Suecia; adult/child €11.50/9; ⏰10.30am-1.30pm & 3.30-5.30pm or 6.15pm Mon-Sat, 10.30am-1.30pm Sun)

Jardines del Real   PARK

4 ◉ MAP P112, B2

Reaching down to the riverbed are the Royal Gardens, a lovely spot for a stroll, with plenty of palms and orange trees as well as a small aviary. Once the grounds of a palace, they're often called Los Viveros. (📞962 08 43 04; www.valencia.es; Calle de San Pío V; ⏰7.30am-9.30pm Apr-Oct, to 8.30pm Nov-Mar)

Las Fallas

The exuberant, anarchic swirl of **Las Fallas de San José** (www.fallas.com; ⊙Mar) – fireworks, music, festive bonfires and all-night partying – is a must if you're visiting Spain in mid-March. It's one of the country's most notable fiestas.

The *fallas* themselves (*falles* in *valenciano*) are huge sculptures of papier mâché, polystyrene and wood built by teams of local artists. Each neighbourhood sponsors its own *falla*, and when the town wakes after the *plantà* (overnight construction of the *fallas*) on the morning of 16 March, more than 350 have sprung up. Reaching up to 15m in height, with the most expensive costing hundreds of thousands of euros, these grotesque, colourful effigies satirise celebrities, current affairs and local customs. They range from comical to moving and Valencians keenly judge the quality of the individual figures, known as *ninots*. Various prizes are on offer for the best *fallas* in each category, and winning the overall prize for best *falla* is a high honour strenuously competed for.

As well as the figures, you can expect all the trappings of a proper Spanish fiesta. Around-the-clock festivities include brass bands waking the city up at 8am, street parties, paella-cooking competitions, parades, open-air concerts, bullfights and free firework displays. Valencia considers itself the pyrotechnic capital of the world and each day at 2pm from 1 to 19 March, a *mascletà* (over five minutes of deafening thumps and explosions) shakes the window panes of Plaza del Ayuntamiento.

But the major pyrotechnics are yet to come, for after midnight on the final day, 19 March, each *falla* goes up in flames – backed by yet more fireworks. So all the admired *ninots* end as charred cinders? All but one: a popular vote spares the most cherished figure, which gets housed for posterity in the Museo Fallero (p87). This is a great place to get a feel for the *fallas* themselves and the evolution of the festival over time as it grew and changed through the 19th and 20th centuries.

Book accommodation well ahead for Las Fallas. Other towns and villages in the Valencian region also have *fallas* celebrations these days, so it's a great time to be in the area.

Fusion Art

YOGA

5 ⊙ MAP P112, D1

This cooperative space can be used by anyone who puts forward a proposal for a regular class or activity or a one-off event or performance. Check online to see what's coming up this month – it might be a Latin dance night, family-oriented painting classes, capoeira, yoga, reiki or a rock concert. Some are designed for monthly subscription, others welcome drop-ins. (☎961 93 95 15; www.facebook.com/fusionartespacio; Calle de Juan Giner 5)

Jardín de Monforte
GARDENS

 6 MAP P112, C3

These under-the-radar ornamental gardens designed in the mid-19th century are a peaceful spot to escape the city. Marble statues, sculpted hedges and a goldfish-filled pond complete the neoclassical style, and walkways shaded by canopies of flowering vines offer welcome relief from the summer heat. The small but grand pavilion at the entrance and its picturesque backdrops make this a popular spot for weddings. (☎963 52 54 78; Plaza de la Legión Española; admission free; ☺10.30am-8pm mid-Mar–mid-Sep, to 6pm mid-Sep–mid-Mar)

Eating

Gran Azul
VALENCIAN €€€

 7 MAP P112, D4

Spacious and stylish, this main-road spot is a temple to excellent dining. Things are focused on rice dishes and the grill, with premium quality steaks from mature cows as well as superb fresh fish simply done and garnished with flair. For a starter, try the *molletes* – mini burgers with fillings such as steak tartare or bull's tail. (☎961 47 45 23; www.granazulrestaurante.com; Avenida de Aragón 12; mains €17-24; ☺1.30-4pm & 8.30-11.30pm Mon-Sat; ☎)

Ricard Camarena
GASTRONOMY €€€

 8 MAP P112, A1

Valencia's most highly rated current chef showcases the range of his abilities in the Bombas Gens (p113) factory turned art centre. A range of tasting menus focuses on the Valencian ideal of fresh market produce, presented in innovative ways that bring out exceptional and subtle flavours. There's a weekday lunchtime set menu for €68. (☎963 35 54 18; www.ricardcamararestaurant.com; Avenida de Burjassot 54; degustation menu €125-155; ☺1.30-3pm & 8-10pm Wed-Sat; ☎)

Balansiya
MOROCCAN €

 9 MAP P112, F2

This restaurant in a student neighbourhood near the university is worth seeking out. Elegantly decorated in Moroccan style, it's a warmly welcoming spot serving a wide range of dishes, including excellent sweets. The aromas will have you instantly slavering. No alcohol served, though there's an unusually long list of nonalcoholic wines. Its homemade hibiscus drink is the way to go. (☎963 89 08 24; www.balansiya.com; Paseo de las Facultades 3; mains €8-13; ☺1.30-4.30pm & 8.30pm-midnight)

KARTINKIN77/SHUTTERSTOCK ©

Jardín de Monforte (p115)

La Vida es Bella

TAPAS €

10 MAP P112, D1

The front terrace and back garden of this innovative spot make great places to relax and absorb Benimaclet life with a beer or bite. More house than restaurant, it exudes a casual charm and heartening enthusiasm. The food is cheerful and presented with a flourish. Burgers, salads and *sartenes* (pan-fried combinations) are all delicious and great value. (📞665 710710; www.facebook.com/lavidaesbellavlc; Calle Mistral 10; dishes €3-11; 🕑8pm-1am Mon-Thu, 12.30-4.30pm & 8pm-1am Fri-Sun)

Tanto Monta

TAPAS €

11 MAP P112, E3

Legendary, tasty and cheap, this place absolutely packs out with students, academics and all comers jostling for a place to enjoy their delicious *montaditos* (tapas snacks on bread). Grab a table outside – if you can – and carefully select a mixed plate. No fighting over who eats what; they're all tops. There are toasts and salads on offer, too. (📞963 29 81 06; Calle del Poeta Artola 19; tapas €2-7; 🕑7pm-1am Mon-Sat; 📶)

El Carabasser

TAPAS €

12 MAP P112, D1

This little tapas place is a very worthwhile eating option in Benimaclet. It packs out – get there early – and no wonder: the *pintxo*-style (skewered Basque tapas) creations coming out of its kitchen are some of the *barrio's* best, and the prices are certainly fair. There's an ecological focus to the food, and vegetarians are well catered for. Best to book. (📞963 89 14 46; www.facebook.com/elcarabasser; Calle Reverendo Rafael Tramoyeres 35; tapas €4-8; ⏰8.45pm-1am; 📶🌱)

Que Ganeta Tinc VALENCIAN €€

13 🍴 MAP P112, E3

White furniture and big windows give a luminous feel to this amiably run restaurant on a lovably bohemian square. It aims more at the university's staff than students, with a pleasing blend of home-style cooking and modern market cuisine. The lunchtime set menu is low-priced at €12 and reliably delicious. There's also an evening set meal (€18). (📞961 13 51 70; http://queganetatinc.es; Plaza Xúquer 4; mains €9-14; ⏰2-4pm & 9-11pm Wed-Sat, 2-4pm Sun; 📶)

Drinking

Deseo 54 GAY & LESBIAN

14 🍸 MAP P112, A1

It's mostly the young and beautiful at this upmarket and famous *discoteca,* which plays quality electronic music to a largely, but by no means exclusively, LGBTIQ+ crowd. Admission prices vary depending on night and DJ, but you can buy cheaper advance tickets on the website. (📞697 699166; www.deseo54.com; Calle de la Pepita 13; ⏰1.30am-7.30am Fri & Sat night; 📶)

Kaf Café CAFE, BAR

15 🍸 MAP P112, D1

Nothing is typical in Benimaclet, but this spot named in homage to Franz Kafka does seem to exemplify the alternative artistic vibe, with regular events and exhibitions of poetry, photography, singer-songwriters and debates. It's a cosy, comfortable place to while away an evening. (📞961 13 17 06; www.facebook.com/kafcafebenimaclet; Calle del Arquitecto Arnau 16; ⏰6pm-1.30am Tue-Sat Sep-Jul; 📶)

Bar Manolo el del Bombo BAR

16 🍸 MAP P112, D3

The Spanish football team's most famous fan is genial Manolo, who follows the team with his drum and is a national legend. His unpretentious bar next to Valencia's stadium is festooned with football scarves and other memorabilia and has plenty of atmosphere on game days. (📞644 862619; www.manoloeldelbombo.com; Plaza Valencia Club de Fútbol; ⏰10am-midnight Tue-Sun)

La Salamandra BAR

17 🍸 MAP P112, E3

Small, atmospheric and intimate, this pub is one of the classics of lively Plaza Xúquer near the university. It's a favourite haunt of academics who appreciate a well-poured gin and tonic and music that was recorded years before their students were even born, but its terrace is also frequented by the young for evening beers. (📞963 60 84 60; Plaza Xúquer 6; ⏰4pm-1.30am Tue-Sun; 📶)

Café Bla Bla BAR

18 🍸 MAP P112, F3

Bla Bla, with its plush red drapery and mirrors, is perfect for a relaxing drink or coffee. Candles flicker, soft music plays, there's a particularly well-stocked bar and staff are affable. It plays the straight man in a zone of boisterous student nightlife. There's an entrance on Plaza de Honduras too. (☎963 55 50 65; Calle de Serpis 62; ☺4pm-2am Tue-Sun; 🛜)

Rumbo 144 CLUB

19 🍸 MAP P112, F4

Get down with the students at this uncomplicated nightclub in the university area. Chart hits, cheapish drinks, late closing and occasional live acts or DJs make it ever popular. Thursday's the big student night; you'll feel ancient if you're 30. Admission price varies depending on night and DJ; you can get in cheaper by registering on www.xceed.me. There are a couple of other nightclub options opposite. (☎963 71 00 25; www.facebook.com/rumbo144vlc; Avenida de Blasco Ibáñez 144; ☺1am-7.30am Wed-Sat night)

Entertainment

Valencia Club de Fútbol FOOTBALL

20 ⭐ MAP P112, D3

The city's principal team, and a major player in Spanish football, with famously demanding fans. A move to a new ground in the city's northwest has been stalled for several years, so for now it's still at Mestalla (p113), an atmospheric, steeply tiered ground close to the centre. You can buy tickets a few weeks in advance through the website. (Estadio de Mestalla; ☎963 37 26 26; www.valenciacf.com; Avenida de Aragón)

Black Note LIVE MUSIC

21 ⭐ MAP P112, D4

Valencia's most active venue for jazz, boogaloo, funk and soul, Black Note has live music around midnight most nights and good canned sounds. It's a well-established, reliable place; admission, including first drink, ranges from free to €15, depending on who's grooving. Wednesday-night jam sessions are always fun. (☎619 394665; www.blacknoteclub.com; Calle Polo y Peyrolón 15; ☺9pm-3.30am Wed-Sat)

Wah Wah LIVE MUSIC

22 ⭐ MAP P112, F4

For many, Wah Wah remains Valencia's hottest venue for live music, especially underground and international indie, though classic Spanish garage and rock also get a good airing. Check the website; tickets are sometimes cheaper if purchased in advance. (www.facebook.com/salawahwah; Calle de Ramón Campoamor 52; ☺10.30pm-3am Thu-Sat Sep-Jun; 🛜)

Valencian Football

Football is big here, and going to a game is a great experience. There are two main teams, which are normally at home on alternate weekends, so there's nearly always a game on from late August to mid-May. Matches can be scheduled any time from Friday night to Monday night, and this isn't decided until a couple of weeks before.

The big brother is **Valencia CF**, in recent decades one of Spain's more successful teams and winners of several Spanish and European trophies. They are one of the world's most supported clubs, with notoriously demanding fans and a strong tradition of developing top players from their own academy.

Levante Unión Deportiva (Estadi Ciutat de València; Map p112, C1; 963 37 95 30; www.levanteud.com; Calle de San Vicente de Paul 44) have fewer resources, are beset with financial problems and have yo-yoed between the top and second divisions. Nevertheless, though the little sibling, they are the older team, having been founded in 1909.

Matisse Club
LIVE MUSIC

23 MAP P112, F4

This atmospheric bar and venue has a varied and interesting programme of cultural happenings, from language exchange to classical music to rock. There's live music of some sort nearly every night and there's always a friendly atmosphere. (685 240014; www.matisseclub.com; Calle de Ramón Campoamor 60; 10pm-3am;)

16 Toneladas
LIVE MUSIC

24 MAP P112, A1

This spacious rock venue down the side of the bus station has regular live acts and also functions as a nightclub. Think €8 to €10 entry. (963 49 45 84; www.16toneladas.com; Calle de Ricardo Micó 3; 10pm-6.30am Fri & Sat, plus concert days;)

Cines Babel
CINEMA

25 MAP P112, D4

Multi-screen Babel shows exclusively undubbed films and runs a pleasant cafe. Admission prices are lower midweek, with Wednesday being substantially discounted. (box office 963 62 67 95; www.cinesalbatrosbabel.com; Calle Vicente Sancho Tello 10; tickets €8.50)

Shopping

Lakajade Vintage
VINTAGE

26 MAP P112, D1

A range of striking items from the '70s and '80s makes this one of the city's best-curated vintage stores. (961 81 56 42; www.lakajadevintage.com; Calle del Arquitecto Arnau 28; 11am-2pm & 5-9pm Mon-Fri, 9am-7pm Sat)

Explore ⊛

Valencia's Seaside

Valencia's town beach is 3km from the centre, a wide strip of sand some 4km long. It's bordered by the Paseo Marítimo promenade and a string of restaurants and cafes. The refurbished port and marina area, popular with cruise ships, is south of here and backed by the intriguing fishermen's district of El Cabanyal, which makes for excellent exploration.

The Short List

o **Playa de la Patacona (p125)** *Sauntering along the beach, gazing out at the Mediterranean towards the Balearic Islands.*

o **Mercat Municipal del Cabanyal (p123)** *Appraising the produce on offer, then taking a stroll through the intriguing fishing barrio (neighbourhood).*

o **Rent Yacht World (p125)** *Getting out on the water and seeing the wind fill the sails.*

o **La Fábrica de Hielo (p128)** *Dancing the afternoon away at this quirky cultural spot.*

Getting There & Around

🚋 Lines 4 and 6 head out to the beach suburbs.

Ⓜ The Marítim-Serrería stop is a short walk from Cabanyal.

🚌 Numerous bus lines head out to the beaches, port area and Cabanyal; 31, 32, 92 and 93 are some of the handier ones.

🚉 The Cabanyal station is a couple of stops from the Estación del Norte on the *cercanía* trains.

Valencia's Seaside Map on p124

El Cabanyal (p122) MOONSTONE IMAGES/GETTY IMAGES ©

Walking Tour 🥾

Strolling Through El Cabanyal

The barrio of El Cabanyal has loads of character, and is packed with interesting facades. This is traditionally where fishing families lived and, though undergoing gradual gentrification, it's still got a very working-class maritime feel to it. It's worth taking your time to stroll around – a jaunt that can easily become a tapas crawl, as there are several worthwhile eating options.

Start Mercat Municipal del Cabanyal; train Valencia-Cabanyal

Finish Bodega La Peseta

Length 1.5km; one hour

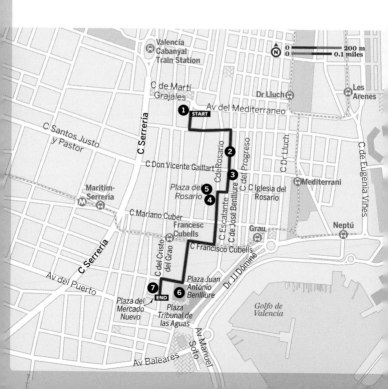

❶ Local Market

Start at the **Mercat Municipal del Cabanyal** (☎963 44 63 16; www.mercadocabanyal.es; Calle de Martí Grajales 4; ⏱7am-2.30pm Mon-Sat). The local women of this fishing *barrio* jostle each other and prod the vegetables in this vibrant local food market. The bar here will cook your purchase for you if you're peckish.

❷ Narrow Streets

Wander southeast into the core of the district. The narrow streets are flanked by extremely pretty centenarian houses, decorated with tiles and flourishes in a vernacular version of the Modernista mansions going up in richer parts of town.

❸ Historic Tavern

One of Valencia's most characterful spots, with the atmosphere of another era, **Bodega Casa Montaña** (☎963 67 23 14; www.emilianobodega.com; Calle de José Benlliure 69; tapas €4-14; ⏱1-4pm & 7.30-11.30pm Mon-Sat, 12.30-4pm Sun) has been around since 1836. There's a superb wine selection and exquisite tapas, including seafood conserves. We loved the smoked eel here, but it's all great. Eat in the bar or the small restaurant (bookings advised).

❹ Plaza del Rosario

This pleasant, tucked-away square is a nice place to sit and watch a bit of *barrio* life pass by. The palm-shaded plaza is dominated by the facade of the local church, and has a community theatre (p129) on it.

❺ Rice Museum

The **Museo de Arroz** (☎962 08 40 75; www.valencia.es; Calle del Rosario 3; adult/child €2/1, Sun free; ⏱10am-2pm & 3-7pm Tue-Sat, 10am-2pm Sun) is a restored rice mill with three levels of complex belts, pulleys and machinery that will enthral those of an engineering bent. There's some info in English, as well as a video that gives a little of the 1000-year history of rice in Valencia. You can investigate the fishers' Holy Week traditions in an adjoining museum.

❻ Gothic Warehouses

Originally constructed in the 14th century in Gothic style, the **Reales Atarazanas** (Les Drassanes del Grau; www.valencia.es; ☎963 52 54 78; Plaza Juan Antonio Benlliure; adult/child €2/1, free Sun; ⏱10am-2pm & 3-6pm or 7pm Tue-Sat, 10am-2pm Sun) are five parallel shipyard warehouses that have been much altered over the years. Their beautifully restored interiors hold exhibitions and a small display on Valencia's maritime history.

❼ Tapas Time

Next to the **Mercado Municipal del Grao** (Plaza del Mercado Nuevo; ⏱7.30am-3pm Mon-Sat) and combining the old, the new and the carefree, **Bodega La Peseta** (☎960 43 15 85; Calle del Cristo del Grao 10; tapas €3-8; ⏱7.30pm-12.30am Wed & Thu, 12.30-5pm & 7.30pm-12.30am Fri-Sun; 📶🍴) is a Cabanyal alternative icon done out in 1970s retro style. Tasty tapas make it a good stop for a drink and a snack.

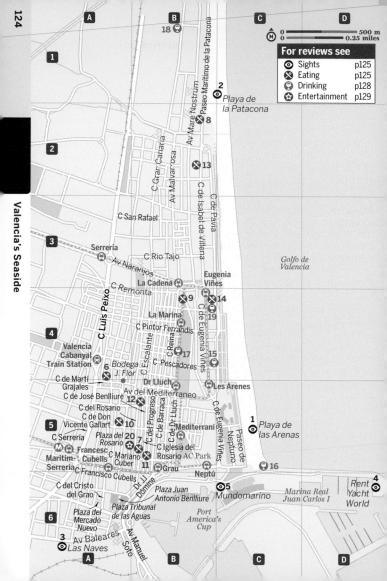

For reviews see

- ◉ Sights — p125
- ✕ Eating — p125
- ⬮ Drinking — p128
- ★ Entertainment — p129

0 — 500 m
0 — 0.25 miles

Map labels:

18

2 — Playa de la Patacona

Paseo Marítimo de la Patacona

Av Mare Nostrum

8

13

C Gran Canaria

Av Malvarrosa

C de Isabel de Villena

C de Pavía

C San Rafael

Golfo de Valencia

3 — Serrería

Av Naranjos

C Río Tajo

La Cadena

Eugenia Viñes

C Remonta

9

14

19

La Marina

C de Eugenia Viñes

C Pintor Ferrandis

C Luis Peixo

C Reina

C Escalante

17

15

Valencia Cabanyal Train Station

Bodega J. Flor

6

C Pescadores

Dr Lluch

Les Arenes

C de Martí Grajales

Av del Mediterráneo

C de José Benlliure

12

C del Rosario

1 — Playa de las Arenas

C de Don Vicente Gallart

10

C del Progreso

C de Baraca

Plaza del Rosario

20

C Serrería

7

Mediterrani

C de Dr Lluch

Francesc Cubells

Mariano Cuber

C Iglesia del Rosario AC Park

Paseo de Neptuno

Maritim-Serrería

11

Grau

Neptú

16

C Francisco Cubells

C de Eugenia Viñes

C del Cristo del Grao

Dr JJ Domine

Plaza Juan Antonio Benlliure

5 — Mundomarino

Marina Real Juan Carlos I

Rent 4 Yacht World

Plaza del Mercado Nuevo

Plaza Tribunal de las Aguas

Port America's Cup

3 — Las Naves

Av Baleares

Av Manuel Soto

Sights

Playa de las Arenas
BEACH

1 MAP P124, C5

Stretching north from the marina, this is the beginning of Valencia's beach, the closest to the centre and the focal point of seaside life. Backed by hotels and rice restaurants, it's a lively, busy strip and a major zone for summer nightlife. The beach is over 100m deep, so there's room even in high summer.

Playa de la Patacona
BEACH

2 MAP P124, C1

The northern stretch of Valencia's main beach has a quieter, more local scene, but still gets busy in summer. It's backed by lovely traditional houses that have been converted into eateries, and there are several appealing *chiringuito* (beach-bar) options on the sand. Like the rest of the strip, it's a wide, flat stretch of beach with plenty of room to move even in peak season.

Las Naves
ARTS CENTRE

3 MAP P124, A6

Down near the docks, this former warehouse space has been turned into a hive of creativity, with art and photography exhibitions, a library, rehearsal spaces and numerous events – everything from climate-change debates to children's theatre and face-painting workshops. (963 91 04 77; www.lasnaves.com; Calle de Joan Verdeguer 16; 8am-9pm Mon-Fri, 9am-2pm Sat)

Rent Yacht World
BOATING

4 MAP P124, D6

With a skipper who is serious about safety but also about fun, this is a great option to get out on a yacht. There are three daily departures for short cruises, or rent it out privately for up to 10 people. Prices include drinks and, for some options, food. They also rent out simple motorboats. Other options might see you take to the Med for a week or more, cruising over to the Balearic islands. (610 211998; www.rentyachtworld.es; Marina Real Juan Carlos I; 1hr/2hr cruise €25/45, 1hr/2hr charter €250/450)

Mundomarino
BOATING

5 MAP P124, C6

Offers a variety of catamaran excursions, from one/three hours sailing (€15/42) to sunset cruises (€22) and swimming trips (€20). You can also rent simple kayaks and snorkelling gear here. (963 81 60 66; www.mundomarino.es; Marina Real Juan Carlos I)

Eating

Bar Cabanyal
SEAFOOD €€

6 MAP P124, A4

Opposite the market in the traditional fishing district, you'd expect a bit of a marine flavour, and indeed the young and enthusiastic team does an excellent line in quality seafood at very reasonable prices. Everything is delicious and it's an upbeat, optimistic spot. Opening hours are extended in summer. (961 33 53 77; www.facebook.com/

Almuerzo – A Valencian Rite

In much of the Spanish-speaking world, *almuerzo* is a word for lunch. But for Valencians, it's a mid-morning bite, and sometimes a very substantial one. Head to traditional bars to experience it – places such as **Bar Flor** (Map p124, A5; ☏ 963 71 20 19; www.restaurante bodegaflor.es; Calle de Martí Grajales 21; ⏱8.30am-5.30pm Mon-Sat) and **La Pascuala** in Cabanyal are typical – and expect to see people downing filled rolls as long as your forearm, or maybe a plate of calamari, accompanied by peanuts, lupin beans and a beer or two. Then a coffee and it's back to work. So it's a kind of brunch then? No, because they'll have lunch afterwards too!

barcabanyal; Calle de Martí Grajales 5; dishes €6-15; ⏱8-11pm Tue, 1-4pm & 8-11pm Wed-Sat, 1-4pm Sun)

Bar La Paca   TAPAS €

 7 ⊗ MAP P124, B5

Cosy and buzzing, this bar has an eclectic crowd and an uplifting atmosphere. Visually striking with its chessboard tiles and deep reds, it does simple, tasty tapas (including vegetarian options) and craft beers at fair prices. It's the sort of place where you wish you lived upstairs. (☏637 860528; Calle del Rosario 30; tapas €3-8; ⏱1pm-1am)

La Más Bonita   CAFE €€

8 ⊗ MAP P124, B2

Pretty in turquoise and white, this idyllically situated beachfront place has comfy outdoor seating, a modern vibe and a big interior and patio. It's a charming venue for breakfast in the sun, or for muffins, cheesecakes or other delicacies any time of day. There's also a terrace right on the promenade and a *chiringuito* on the sand itself. (☏961 14 36 11; www.lamasbonita. es; Paseo Marítimo de la Patacona 11; pastries €3-7, light meals €6-15; ⏱8am-1.30am; 🛜)

La Pascuala   SANDWICHES €

9 ⊗ MAP P124, B4

This legendary Cabanyal business is famed for its huge *bocadillos* (filled rolls) that come absolutely stuffed with fillings. Half of Valencia seems to be in here around 11am for a mid-morning try. There's a huge selection; try the Super, which includes horse meat, traditional in parts of Spain and on the rise for its healthy qualities. (☏963 71 38 14; www.facebook.com/bodegalapascuala; Calle de Doctor Lluch 299; half/whole roll €3.10/6.20; ⏱9am-3.30pm Mon-Sat)

Bodega Anyora   TAPAS €€

10 ⊗ MAP P124, A5

An evocation of old Valencia through a modern design eye, this rehabilitated old bodega is visually lovely, with gleaming handmade tiles, a traditional floor and fresco vegetables on the walls.

It does snacks to accompany your vermouth as well as quality fuller plates, which are based on nose-to-tail local tradition with a few modern twists and something for vegetarians, too. (📞963 55 88 09; www.facebook.com/anyorabodega; Calle de Don Vicente Gallart; dishes €6-13; ⏱1-3.30pm & 8-11pm Tue-Sat)

Casa Guillermo TAPAS €€

11 ❌ MAP P124, B5

This renowned Cabanyal spot has a stratospheric reputation for its anchovies, which are very tasty, if rather pricey. Other dishes, such as fish croquettes or mussels, are delicious and more compassionately priced. (📞963 67 91 77; www.casaguillermo1957.com; Calle del Progreso 15; tapas €5-16; ⏱9.30am-3.30pm & 7.30-11.30pm Mon-Sat; 📶)

Ca la Mar TAPAS €

12 ❌ MAP P124, B5

Informal and down to earth, this local gem is typical of the Cabanyal district. There's a cheerful scene at the outdoor tables, with tasty seafood and other tapas at knock-down prices. (📞963 25 98 27; www.facebook.com/calamarcabanyal; Calle de Just Vilar 19; tapas €4-9; ⏱11am-1am Tue, Wed & Fri-Sun, 9am-1am Thu)

Casa Carmela VALENCIAN €€

13 ❌ MAP P124, B2

One of Valencia's best paellas. The expansive restaurant has been serving rice since 1922 and remains a favourite with families. Huge paellas are cooked over an orange-wood fire and served with a traditional wooden spoon. (📞963 71 00 73; www.casa-carmela.com; Calle de Isabel de Villena 155; paella per person €18; ⏱1-4pm Tue-Sun)

La Lonja del Pescado SEAFOOD €€

14 ❌ MAP P124, B4

One block back from the beach at Malvarrosa, this busy, informal place has plenty of atmosphere and offers decent value, specialising in traditional fried seafood and fish. Grab an order form as you enter and fill it in at your table. The Eugenia Viñes tram stop is right outside. (📞963 55 35 35; Calle de Eugenia Viñes 243; dishes €8-16; ⏱8.30-11pm Tue-Thu, 1.30-4.30pm & 8.30-11pm Fri-Sun May-Sep, 1.30-4pm & 8.30-11pm Fri & Sat, 1.30-4pm Sun Oct-Apr)

Playa de la Malvarrosa

VON SCHONERTAGEN/ISTOCK EDITORIAL/GETTY IMAGES ©

Drinking

La Fábrica de Hielo   CAFE

15 🚇 MAP P124, B4

It's difficult to know how to classify this former ice factory, converted with charm into a multi-purpose space that does cultural events, drinks and tapas just back from the beach. Drop by and see – Sundays are fun, with paella and dancing, but there's always a great atmosphere. (📞963 68 26 19; www.lafabricadehielo. net; Calle de Pavia 37; ⏰5pm-midnight Mon, 5pm-1am Tue-Thu, to 1.30am Fri, 11am-1.30am Sat, to midnight Sun)

Marina Beach Club   BAR

16 🚇 MAP P124, C5

A superpopular bar and club with two restaurants at an enviable loca-

La Fábrica de Hielo

tion overlooking the sand between Valencia's marina and Playa de las Arenas. The open-air space features palm trees, an infinity pool and stunning views. A hit with locals and visitors, it gets particularly crowded in the height of summer. (📞961 15 00 07; http://marinabeachclub.com; Marina Real Juan Carlos I; ⏰11am-3.30am)

La Batisfera   BAR

17 🚇 MAP P124, B4

This interesting space combines a bookshop, which has a great English selection and a secondhand section, with an upbeat bar-cafe that often has live music and other events. It's a family-friendly spot with a kids' play area. (📞962 04 58 45; www.labatisfera.com; Calle Carlos Ros 32; ⏰bar 5pm-1am Mon, noon-1am Wed, Thu & Sun, to 2.30am Fri & Sat; 👶)

La Casa de la Mar   BAR

18 🚇 MAP P124, B1

This cavernous warehouse a block from the beach is a surfing school (p25), bar, yoga studio, mini skate park and small coworking space. The surfer vibe continues in the menu, with açaí and poke bowls, juices, salads and sandwiches. Deckchairs and long benches on artificial grass make this a great spot for a Sunday session. Also hosts live music. (www.lacasadelamar.com; Avenida Vicente Blasco Ibáñez Novelista 8; ⏰10am-10pm Tue-Sun May-Sep, 5-10pm Thu, 5-11pm Fri, 9am-11pm Sat, 10am-11pm Sun Oct-Apr)

Food Fight!

The last Wednesday in August marks Spain's messiest festival. **La Tomatina** (www.latomatina.info; tickets €12) is a tomato-throwing orgy attracting more than 20,000 visitors to Buñol, a town of just 9000 inhabitants. At 11am, more than 100 tonnes of squishy tomatoes are tipped from trucks to the waiting crowd. For one hour, everyone joins in a cheerful, anarchic tomato battle.

Participation costs €12 through the official website, though numerous tour operators offer tickets and packages from Valencia, Alicante and elsewhere. There are cloakroom facilities on site, as you can't take bags or cameras into the festival area. Bring a set of fresh clothes to change into afterwards. In the Tomatina itself, some people choose a pair of goggles to protect their eyes. Flip-flops don't work very well; you're better off with shoes, but don't expect them to be clean again.

If you buy a package, try to opt out of the 'paella and sangría' add-ons, as these are readily available for less on the street. While most visitors just come in from Valencia for the event, it can be worthwhile staying over the night before and after. La Tomatina is one element of the locals' main fiesta and there's plenty of atmosphere, as well as concerts, across a whole week. On the Saturday before the Tomatina, there's a version for four- to 14-year-olds, which is free to enter.

Akuarela Playa

CLUB

19 🚇 MAP P124, B4

A huge space in a historic villa complex, this is a typical summer nightclub, with an outdoor section. Right by the beach, it's a classic of the Valencian hot season. The music is very commercial – mainly Spanish and Latin pop and pachanga hits. (🖉645 145221; www.akuarelaplaya.es; Calle de Eugenia Viñes 152; 🕐1-7.30am Mon-Sat nights, 6pm-midnight Sun Jun-Sep; 🛜)

Entertainment

Teatre El Musical

THEATRE

20 ⭐ MAP P124, A5

With an outrageously tall door, this theatre is by a church in the heart of the Cabanyal *barrio* and offers a community-involved programme of theatre, dance, recitals and comedy, with some events suitable for young children. There's also a good cafe-bar. (🖉962 08 56 91; www.teatreelmusical.es; Plaza del Rosario 3; 👫)

Explore ◈

Western Valencia

Spanning a broad swath of suburbs west of the old town, this neighbourhood has varied attractions. At the western end of the Turia riverbed, the Bioparc zoo presents African animals in innovative ways, while the museum of local history gives an overview of the city's past. Various park spaces across the area give a pleasant timeout from urban life.

The Short List

○ **Bioparc (p133)** *Getting up close and personal with the lemurs at this unusual zoo devoted to African animals.*

○ **Jardín Botánico (p133)** *Strolling peacefully around this fairly central green space run by the University of Valencia.*

○ **Bar Ricardo (p134)** *Snacking on something fishy with an expertly poured beer at this wonderfully traditional tapas bar.*

○ **Loco Club (p137)** *Catching a band at this atmospheric and well-respected venue.*

Getting There & Around

🚌 The area is served by lots of bus lines, including the 95, which runs along either side of the Turia to its end near the Bioparc.

Ⓜ The closest stop to the Bioparc is Nou d'Octubre, about 800m away.

🚲 It's an easy ride along the Turia riverbed to the attractions in the west of the area.

Western Valencia Map on p132

Jardín Botánico (p133) PETRAPHOTO/SHUTTERSTOCK ©

Western Valencia

For reviews see

Sights	p133
Eating	p134
Drinking	p135
Entertainment	p137
Shopping	p137

0 — 500 m
0 — 0.25 miles

RUSSAFA

Gran Vía
Germanies

C de Colón

Av del Marqués de Sotelo

Av Bailén

C de San Vicente Mártir

SOUTH
CIUTAT
VELLA

NORTH
CIUTAT
VELLA

Plaza del
Mercado

C Alta (Dalt)

C de Pere
Bonfill

C de Dr Sanchis
Bergón

Bus Station

Av de Menéndez
Pidal

C del Turia

Jardín
Botánico

C de Guillem de Castro

C de Quart

C Murillo

Av Oeste

C de San Vicente Mártir

C del
Hospital

C de Guillem
de Castro

Angel
Guimerá

Gran Vía Ramón y Cajal

Plaza de
España

C Jesús

Pasaje de
Ventura Feliú

Estación
Joaquín
Sorolla

Jesús

C de Albacete

C Cuenca

C de San José
de Calasanz

Av Giorgeta

C Cuenca

C Beato
Nicolás Factor

C Tres Forques

Av Salavert

C Archiduque Carlos

Av de Pío XII

Av Maestro
Rodrigo

C Valle de la
Ballestera

Puente
Ademuz

Av de Tirso
de Molina

Av de Pío Baroja

Bioparc

Parque de
Cabecera

Puente de
Campanar

Jardín de las
Hespérides

Paseo de la Pechina

Jardines
del Turia

C de Gaspar
Bono

C de Juan Llorens
de la Montaña

C de San José

C del Turia

Gran Vía Fernando
el Católico

C de
Lepanto

C del
Guillem Sorolla

C de Quart

C de Gabriel Miró

C Carlos III

Calixto III

C del Erudito
Orellana

Ángel Guimerá

C de Sueca

C de Buen Orden

C Salvador Ferrandis Luna

C del Cid

C Brasil

C Linares

Av Pérez Galdós

C Enguera

C del Cid

C Castán Tobeñas

C de Valencia

Puente 9 de
Octubre

Museo de
Historia de
Valencia

Nou
d'Octubre

C Santa Cruz de Tenerife

C Músico Ayllón

C Tres Forques

C José María Mortes Lerma

Av Tres Cruces

Av de los
Tamarindos

Sights

Bioparc ZOO

1 ◉ MAP P132, B1

This zoo devoted solely to African animals has an educational and conservationist remit and an unusual approach. Though, as always, the confinement of creatures such as gorillas in limited spaces raises mixed feelings, the innovative landscaping is certainly a thrill. The absence of obvious fences makes it seem that animals roam free as you wander from savannah to equatorial landscapes. Aardvarks, leopards and hippos draw crowds, but most magical is Madagascar, where large-eyed lemurs gambol around your feet near waterfalls and grass. (☑ 960 66 05 26; www.bioparcvalencia.es; Avenida de Pío Baroja 3; adult/child €24/18; ☺ 10am-dusk; 👪)

Museo de Historia de Valencia MUSEUM

2 ◉ MAP P132, A2

This museum is very well presented and plots more than 2000 years of Valencia's history (p136). Each period is illustrated with a display case, making the visit a little like window shopping. It's an atmospheric, brick-pillared, crypt-like space in a 19th-century water deposit. As usual, the elephant in the room is the Civil War, which merits only 20 lines, even though Valencia was republican Spain's capital for some of it. Panels are in Spanish/valenciano, but there are multilingual information folders

available. (☑ 963 70 11 78; http://mhv.valencia.es; Calle de Valencia 42; adult/child €2/1, Sun free; ☺ 10am-7pm Tue-Sat, to 2pm Sun)

Jardín Botánico GARDENS

3 ◉ MAP P132, D1

Established in 1802, this was Spain's first botanic garden. With mature trees and plants, an extensive cactus garden and a wary colony of feral cats, the walled garden run by the University of Valencia is a shady, tranquil place to relax. Check the website for evening jazz concerts. (☑ 963 15 68 00; www.jardibotanic.org; Calle de Quart 80; adult/child €2.50/1.50; ☺ 10am-9pm May-Aug, to 8pm Apr & Sep, to 7pm Mar & Oct, to 6pm Nov-Feb)

Jardín de las Hespérides GARDENS

4 ◉ MAP P132, D1

Abutting the botanical gardens, this modern creation could not be more distinct in style. Shorter on green space, it has the formality of a classic French garden with cypresses, low banks of herbs, and staggered terraces where tangy citrus trees flourish. (Paseo de la Pechina; admission free; ⏰10am-6pm Nov-Mar, 10am-8pm Apr-Oct)

Eating

Bar Ricardo
TAPAS €€

5 MAP P132, D1

Ice-cold beer and a fabulous array of tapas and other dishes characterise this gloriously traditional place, with its old-style mezzanine, pleasant terrace and top-notch service. Snails, top-quality seafood, one of Valencia's best *cañas* (small draught beers) and many other delights await you. The kitchen is open all day, so it's a good spot for eating outside of normal Spanish hours. (📞963 22 69 49; www.barricardo.es; Calle de Doctor Zamenhof 16; mains €10-18; ⏰8am-midnight Tue-Sat Sep-Jul)

Bar Rausell
VALENCIAN €€

6 MAP P132, D3

Blending traditional and modern decor, Bar Rausell is dearly loved by locals for its fabulous tapas at the long bar and excellent sit-down food in the restaurant. Cold morsels are on display and reliably excellent traditional and avant-garde bites are cooked to order. The seafood is spectacularly good, and rices very tasty. (📞963 84 31 93; www.rausell.es; Calle Ángel Guimerà 61; mains €12-20; ⏰8.30am-4pm & 8pm-midnight Wed-Sat, 9am-4pm Sun)

El Pederniz
SPANISH €€

7 MAP P132, E4

A warm, genuine welcome and lots of enthusiasm give a great first impression at this comfortably decorated restaurant in a nondescript area, a short hop from the fast-train station. Delicious seafood and game dishes make for a reliably excellent experience. It's a good option for a leisurely lunch before catching a train, but worth seeking out in any case. (📞963 32 41 06; www.elpederniz.com; Pasaje de Ventura Feliú 20; mains €11-22; ⏰1-4.30pm & 8.30-11pm Mon & Wed-Sat, 1-4.30pm Tue; 📶)

Pelegrí
VALENCIAN €€

8 MAP P132, E2

A little off the centre's tourist beat, this refined spot makes a fine lunch stop. The husband-and-wife team offer a choice of three set menus (and a short à la carte menu) that are brilliant value for food that's beautifully conceived and presented without losing the comfort factor. Interesting wines round out the meal. (📞963 91 63 40; www.restaurantepelegrivalencia.com; Calle de Lepanto 23; set menus €16-22; ⏰1-4pm & 9-11pm Tue-Sat, 1-4pm Sun)

La Greta
TAPAS €

9 MAP P132, E1

Offering an eye-catchingly original environment – all quirky retro design – La Greta has a very pleasing menu of tapas and plates designed to share, with lots of vegetarian

SCULPTOR: FERNANDO GONZÁLEZ SITGES;

Bioparc (p133)

choice and quite a bit of Lebanese influence. Portions are generous and service welcoming. (📞963 32 24 47; Calle de Pere Bonfill 7; dishes €4-12; 🕙6pm-1am year-round, 1-6pm Sat & Sun Oct-May; 📶🌱)

Pastelería Dulce de Leche   CAFE €

10 🍴 MAP P132, E4

Always busy, this *barrio* (neighbourhood) patisserie-cafe does a splendid range of delicious cakes; it's pretty tough to choose. There are also decent savoury options, including a daily pasta special. Order at the counter, then take your number to a table. (📞960 11 23 16; www.pasteleriadulcedeleche.com; Calle de Jesús 71; light meals €3-8; 🕙8am-9pm Mon-Sat, 8.30am-9pm Sun)

Mercado San Vicente   MARKET €€

11 🍴 MAP P132, E4

This was still under construction when we last passed by, but should be worth a look. Due to open in 2021, it's a new gastromarket designed along the lines of Madrid's famous Mercado San Miguel. Stalls in the former printing factory near the train station will sell quality produce and provide tapas. (Calle Maestro Sosa 21)

Drinking

La Fábrica de Huellas   CAFE

The 'footprint factory' (see 14 ⭐ Map p132, E1) is a dog-friendly cafe where you can bring furry friends or make new ones over an organic coffee. There is always a

Valencia: A Brief History of the City

Pensioned-off Roman legionaries founded 'Valentia' on the banks of Río Turia in 138 BCE, but the first city was destroyed by Pompey in 75 BCE due to the Sertorian War.

The Moors made Valencia an agricultural and industrial centre, establishing ceramics, paper, silk and leather industries and extending the network of irrigation canals in the rich agricultural hinterland. Muslim rule was briefly interrupted in 1094 CE by the rampage of the legendary Castilian knight El Cid. Much later, the Christian forces of Jaime I definitively retook the city in 1238 after a siege. The city finally surrendered and tens of thousands of Muslims were displaced.

Valencia's golden age was the 15th and early-16th centuries, when the city was one of the Mediterranean's strongest trading centres. Commerce brought wealth and magnificent buildings. However, the expulsion of the Jews, then the *moriscos* (converted Muslims) from Spain left this formerly multicultural city bereft of citizens and important sectors of society. Meanwhile, New World discoveries led to a Spanish pivot towards the Atlantic, beginning Sevilla's pre-eminence as a trading city and hastening Valencia's decline. Economic hardship led to the Germanías revolt (1519–22) of the guilds against the crown and aristocracy. Several lean centuries ensued, finally relieved in the 19th century by industrialisation and the development of a lucrative citrus trade to northern Europe.

Loyalist Valencia was the capital of republican Spain during an important part of the Spanish Civil War, after the government abandoned Madrid, fearing it was about to fall to the Nationalists. In the war's traumatic final days, the city surrendered and a period of harsh repression and poverty ensued, not helped by severe floods in 1949 and 1957 that led to the Río Turia being diverted away from the city centre. The dry riverbed was eventually converted into a park, Jardines del Turia.

The return to democracy brought regional semi-autonomy and a huge injection of confidence to Valencia. Though the city went bankrupt in the global financial crisis, a casualty of rampant corruption and overborrowing, things are on the up and the vibrancy and optimism of daily life here is always remarkable.

welcoming resident dog to quickly adopt whoever comes through the door. Part of the animal-therapy-focused ACAVALL Foundation, the cafe also has an area housing cats available for adoption that everyone (except the pooches) can visit. (961 93 06 79; www.lafabricade huellas.com; Calle del Turia 60; 9am-2pm & 5-10pm Tue-Sun)

Pub Bubu   GAY

12 🚇 MAP P132, D2

Haven't shaved since the holiday started? Not a problem at all here at this notably friendly bear den. The inclusive atmosphere makes anybody feel at home. (📞696 607626; www.bubupub.com; Calle Botánico 7; ⏰8pm-3.30am Thu-Sat; 📶)

Entertainment

Loco Club   LIVE MUSIC

13 ⭐ MAP P132, D2

This popular, long-established venue puts on bands and solo acts, usually between Thursday and Saturday. Entry, depending on the band of the day, is €5 to €20. Some gigs are free for under-25s. (📞963 51 85 21; www.lococlub.es; Calle del Erudito Orellana 12; ⏰9pm-3am Thu-Sat & other concert days)

Café del Duende   LIVE PERFORMANCE

14 ⭐ MAP P132, E1

This intimate spot has decent, reasonably authentic flamenco performances four nights a week. It's quite small, so it's worth queuing up before the show starts to avoid disappointment. Shows last about an hour. (📞630 455289; http://cafedelduende.com; Calle del Turia 62; entry incl drink €12; ⏰shows 10.30pm Thu, 11pm Fri & Sat, 8pm Sun; 📶)

Teatro la Estrella   PUPPETRY

15 ⭐ MAP P132, D1

This puppet theatre puts on weekend shows aimed at families.

It's a rather enchanting spot, and you can see some of the puppets displayed beforehand. Some shows are more suited to non-Spanish-speaking kids than others though, so it's probably best to ask first. It runs another theatre in the Cabanyal district near the beach. (Sala Petxina; 📞963 56 22 92; www.teatrolaestrella.com; Calle del Doctor Sanchis Bergón 29; tickets €6-8; 👶)

Shopping

100% Pirata   FASHION & ACCESSORIES

16 🔒 MAP P132, D3

There is another branch in the centre, but we prefer this, the original shop, in the western part of the city. The range of breezy women's clothing shows plenty of originality and the designs draw from nature and multiethnic sources. It also does a nice line in leather wallets and other accessories. (📞963 84 37 65; www.100pirata.com; Calle Ángel Guimerà 41; ⏰10am-9pm Mon-Sat)

Vinyl Eye   CLOTHING

17 🔒 MAP P132, E1

This very cool shop has a range of prints with original designs inspired by rock bands, other musical influences and more. Different edgy artists exhibit here and you can get T-shirts and bags printed with any of the motifs that you like. There are occasional concerts and other events. (📞961 47 80 33; www.vinyl-eye.com; Calle del Turia 35; ⏰10am-2pm & 5-8.30pm Mon-Fri, 10am-2pm Sat)

Walking Tour 🥾

The Turia Riverbed

Congratulate the town planners who, when they diverted the Turia away from the city centre to avoid devastating flooding, decided to make the riverbed into a park instead of a six-lane bypass. The glorious park is busy any time of day with dog-walkers, joggers, strollers, playgrounders and romancers. It's a great snapshot of everyday Valencian life; it's worth walking its full 9km length.

Start Ciudad de las Artes y las Ciencias

Finish Parque de Cabecera

Length 9km; two to 2½ hours.

🚌 Number 35, takes you to the southern end of the park from Plaza del Ayuntamiento.

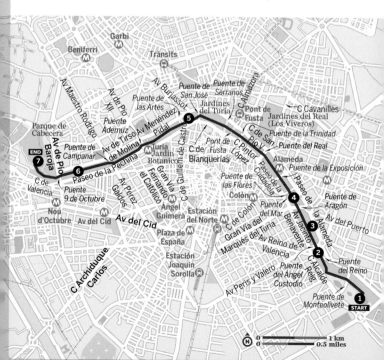

❶ Getting Active

Start your walk at the magnificent buildings of the **Ciudad de las Artes y las Ciencias** (p80). But is it going to be a walk? Your other options include cycle hire or a continuous running track with built-in gradients and distance markers. Regularly spaced public exercise machines offer another option to work off the tapas.

❷ Gulliver

While the whole of the Turia could be considered Valencia's playground, there's nothing to compare with the giant **Gulliver** (⏰10am-8pm Sep-Jun, 10am-2pm & 5-9pm Jul & Aug; 🚼; 🚌19, 95), which just asks to be clambered all over. This giant recumbent man has ropes to climb, slides and more. It's a lovely scene for young kids, with an adjacent skate park to keep the older ones happy.

❸ Musical Landmark

A major city landmark, the **Palau de la Música** (☎963 37 50 20, box office ☎902 010 284; www.palau valencia.com; Paseo de la Alameda 30), perched right over the dry riverbed, is an attractive concert hall hosting mainly classical-music recitals. That long glass tube looks good, but it can get pretty hot under there on a summer's day.

❹ Beautiful Bridges

One of the most attractive of the Turia's old bridges, the elegant stone Renaissance span of the **Puente del Mar** was commissioned in 1591; pride of place goes to images of the Virgin Mary and St Pascual Baylón. Shortly beyond, the **Puente de las Flores** is decorated with 27,000 flowerpots along its sides.

❺ The Oval Ball

While football always grabs the local headlines, there's quite a devoted rugby following in Valencia, and a flourishing local league. The most spectacularly set of the city's grounds is here in the riverbed itself.

❻ Watercourses

Water lore is a major part of Valencian culture, and the eight *acequías* (irrigation canals) that were diverted from the Río Turia to keep the market gardens watered are legendary. At the **Azud de Rovella**, a dam-like structure, you can see where (before the river's course was changed) the last of them, the Rovella, diverted water from the main flow.

❼ City Parkland

At the end of the Turia dry riverbed, the landscaped **Parque de Cabecera** (admission free; ⏰24hr) has a grassy mound to climb for views, plus paths stretching along a stream connecting two small lakes. It's a great spot for strolling, for a jaunt in a swan-shaped pedalo, or for hearing the odd African animal in the adjacent **Bioparc** (p133).

Worth a Trip 🔭
Wander the Wetlands of La Albufera

Synonymous with rice, agriculture and the good-ness of Valencian soil, this lagoon and surrounding flatlands sit just south of Valencia city. Long used for rice cultivation, it's the spiritual home of paella and similar dishes. It has important dune and wet-land ecosystems and its rural ambience, beaches, birdwatching and rustic restaurants make it a great escape, easily accessed by bus or bike.

★ Getting There

🚌 Year-round bus lines 14 and 15 reach Pinedo, while the 25 hits El Saler, some continuing to El Palmar.

El Saler

With long beaches backed by low pine-covered dunes, this appealingly low-key Albufera locale has campsites, hotel and hostel accommodation and a line of restaurants. There are boat trips on the lagoon offered from a dock across a bridge over the main bypass road.

Mirador El Pujol

Though no secret, this viewpoint – a boat dock with jetties extending into the principal lagoon of the Albufera – is still a magical place. It's a handy birdwatching spot, but comes into its own at sunset, when it's gloriously romantic, with herons slowly flapping against the reddening sky. You can take boat trips on the lagoon from here. The viewpoint is at Km 9.5 on the CV500; bus 25 stops right here.

Birdwatching

Birdwatching is good right across the area – on the main lagoon, smaller marshy wetlands and along the coast. Around 90 bird species regularly nest in the zone and more than 250 others use it as a migratory staging post. The **Centro de Interpretación Racó de l'Olla** (963 86 80 50; www.parquesnaturales.gva.es; Carretera El Palmar, Km 0; admission free; 9am-2pm), on the left just after you take the turnoff to El Palmar, has some information on species and a birdwatching area.

El Palmar

The most emblematic of the Albufera settlements, this traditional farming village prides itself as being the birthplace of the Valencian rice dish, and these days every second building seems to be a restaurant serving it: it's ridiculously easy to end up with a quality bellyful. Boat excursions leaving from here typically include a visit to a rice farm as well as a trip on the lagoon. Think €20 for up to four passengers.

★ **Top Tips**

○ Rice is a lunchtime dish, so it makes sense to get here for that, stroll it off in the afternoon, then enjoy the evening birdwatching and spectacular sunset.

○ An extensive cycle lane and flat terrain make exploring La Albufera by bike a top option.

✕ **Take a Break**

There are numerous rice restaurants: **El Sequer de Tonica** (961 62 02 24; www.elsequerdetonica.com; Calle Redolins 85, El Palmar; rice dishes per person €10-16; 10am-4.30pm Wed-Mon, plus 7-11pm Fri & Sat summer;) is one of our favourites.

Worth a Trip 🔭
See the Views from Hilltop Castillo de Sagunto

Sagunto, 25km north of Valencia, offers spectacular panoramas over orange groves to the coast and the Balearic Islands from its hilltop castle. The majestically located castle's long stone walls girdle twin hilltops. The fortress could do with a facelift and is best for a stroll among the ruins, enjoying the magnificent vistas, rather than learning history. Don't expect interpretative panels or audio guides.

📞 962 61 71 67

www.aytosagunto.es

admission free

🕙 10am-6pm or 8pm Tue-Sat, 10am-2pm Sun

A Long History

Its history began with a thriving Iberian community called (infelicitously, with hindsight) Arse. In 219 BCE Hannibal destroyed it, sparking the Second Punic War. Rome won, named the town Saguntum and rebuilt it. The Moors gave the castle its current form; it was later embellished by the Christians and fought over in the Peninsular War.

The Eastern Hilltop

The entrance is on the eastern hilltop, where the Roman town was located. Around the excavated ruins of the forum, you can see the stairs and foundations of a Republican temple. This area is the Plaza de Armas, heart of the medieval castle. From here, Puerta de Almenara leads to the fortified eastern compound.

Carved Stones

Between the two hilltops, the Museo de Epigrafía is a collection of engraved stones found on the site. There are Latin funerary and honorary inscriptions, some column capitals and a few stones inscribed in Hebrew from the medieval era. There's some quite interesting information on Roman customs, but it's not in English.

The Western Hilltop

The western hilltop was the site of the original Iberian city, but what you can see here is mostly later fortifications from the 18th and 19th centuries. The most impressive sight is one particularly sturdy bastion, and the views are stirring.

Restored Theatre

Below the castle, you can visit the Roman theatre. An overzealous restoration has resulted in a gigantic stage building and marble seating, which are great for staging performances, but largely devoid of historical atmosphere.

★ Top Tips

o There are a couple of unremarkable options in Sagunto itself, but most accommodation clusters in the beach and port area (Puerto de Sagunto) 5km to the east.

✕ Take a Break

Handily there's a bunch of restaurants, several of them quite decent, on the road winding up to the castle from the Plaza Mayor.

There is no food or refreshments at the castle itself.

★ Getting There

🚃 The best option from Valencia to Sagunto is taking the *cercanía* trains on lines C5 and C6 (one way €3.70, 30 minutes, regular departures).

🚗 Access to the castle by car is difficult because of a residents' zone, so be prepared to walk up.

Worth a Trip 🔭
Uncover Layers of History at Xàtiva

This sprawling hilltop castle offers plenty of history and inspiring views that make a worthwhile day trip from Valencia. Though much modified over the years, the layers of history here are evident, and the precinct has an appealingly Mediterranean feel, with sunbaked stone, olives and pine trees on the rocky hill. In general, there's good, mostly multilingual information throughout.

📞 962 27 42 74
www.xativaturismo.com
adult/child €2.40/1.20
🕙 10am-6pm Tue-Sun Nov-Mar, to 7pm Apr-Oct

Castillo Menor

Above and behind you as you enter, this is the oldest part of the castle, having been an Iberian fortification before being controlled and further fortified by the Carthaginians then Romans. Hannibal took the fortress, and sources say that his Spanish wife Imilce gave birth to the couple's son here. It's a strong bastion, with a Gothic entranceway, medieval battlements and some 20th-century refurbishment.

Castillo Mayor

Ahead of you as you come through the entrance door, the Castillo Mayor is the main part of the castle and stretches away and upwards along the hilltop. It was first fortified by the Romans, who connected it to the Castillo Menor with walls. If you think it's big today, imagine what it must have looked like 300 years ago at full size. Sadly, it was badly damaged by an earthquake in 1748 and never really recovered.

Sala de los Borjas

A construction of the last century, when the fortress was owned by a local paper magnate, this has rooms conserved from the period and, more interestingly, an exhibition on the famous Borja (Borgia) dynasty, particularly the popes.

Prison

The lockup where the Count of Urgel died is one of the castle's most atmospheric spaces, a vaulted dungeon with thick walls and little hope of escape. Jaime was one of a long line of nobles who found themselves detained here during turbulent centuries in Aragonese dynastic politics.

Torre de la Fe

Literally the high point of the castle, the tower offers stunning vistas on both sides and was the heart of the upper castle. From here, the spine of the ridge continues to a ruined watchtower.

★ Top Tip

○ The castle is quite exposed to the sun, so take a hat and water. Drinks are available on site.

✕ Take a Break

In the old town, **La Picaeta de Carmeta** (☑ 619 511971; Plaça de Mercat 19; mains €13-19; ☺ 1.30-4pm daily, plus 8.30pm-midnight Fri & Sat) is an appealing restaurant. **Casa la Abuela** (☑ 962 27 05 25; Calle de la Reina 17; mains €15-20; ☺ 8.30am-3.45pm & 8.30-10.45pm Mon & Thu-Sat, 8.30am-3.45pm Tue, 1-3.45pm Sun) does hearty traditional Valencian cuisine.

★ Getting There

🚆 Frequent C2 *cercanía* trains connect Xàtiva with Valencia (€4.35, 45 minutes, half-hourly); most Valencia–Madrid trains stop here too.

🚶 It's a long (2km) but pleasant uphill walk from town to the castle. If mobility is an issue, save your strength for the castle, which has lots of steps, and get a taxi or the tourist train.

Survival Guide

Before You Go

Book Your Stay

o Valencia has a good range of hotels, with a growing number of central boutique choices.

o There's a huge quantity of central apartments, which are overwhelming some districts completely. Locals complain many lack appropriate planning permissions,

o Lots of hostels cluster around the city centre.

o Hotel prices have risen sharply in Valencia in the last few years, as Spain's tourism boom has seen more visitor numbers.

Best Budget

Russafa Youth Hostel (www.russafayouth hostel.com) Welcoming, intimate and in tapas central.

Home Youth Hostel (www.homehostels valencia.com) Opposite the Lonja, with top facilities.

Red Nest Hostel (www.nesthostels valencia.com) Cheerful,

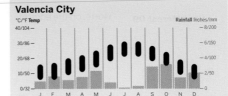

Valencia City

When to Go

o **Spring (Mar-May)** Wonderful time to visit, with good but not oppressive weather, the staggering Las Fallas festival and more.

o **Summer (Jun-Aug)** Hot but enjoyable, with lots of action in the beachfront area and hedonism in the air.

o **Autumn (Sep-Nov)** Temperatures are still normally very pleasant, and the crowds have dropped off.

o **Winter (Dec-Feb)** Valencia's cold season isn't cold by European standards, so don't be put off visiting at this time.

modern and social hostel.

Quart Youth Hostel (www.quarthostel.com) Top facilities and an urban vibe.

Best Midrange

Hostal Antigua Morellana (www.hostalam. com) Great value, family-run spot in the old town.

Ad Hoc Monumental (www.adhochoteles. com) Comfort and charm in a quiet old quarter corner.

Hotel Sorolla Centro

(www.hotelsorolla centro.com) Top value in a winningly central spot without traffic.

Ad Hoc Carmen (www. adhochoteles.com) Handsome modern rooms in an ideal spot.

Hostal Venecia (www. hotelvenecia.com) Right on the main square, this offers modernity and location.

Best Top End

Caro Hotel (www. carohotel.com) Valencia's most enchanting hotel sits on archaeological remains.

One Shot Mercat 09
(www.hoteloneshot
mercat09.com) Near
the market, this per-
sonal, intimate place is
a Valencia standout.

Marqués House (www.
marqueshouse.com)
Modern stylings in a
central historic building.

Hotel Balandret (www.
balandret.com) Stylish
boutique beach hotel.

Arriving in Valencia

Aeropuerto de Valencia (Manises)

Metro lines 3 and 5
connect the airport
with central Valencia. A
taxi into the city centre
costs €25 to €30 (in-
cluding a supplement
for journeys originat-
ing at the airport).
The return journey is
around €15 to €20.

Estación Joaquín Sorolla

Most train travellers
will arrive here. A free
shuttle bus runs to

nearby Estación del
Norte, on the edge of
the old town and on
major bus routes. A taxi
from either to destina-
tions around the centre
will cost €4 to €7.

Estación de Autobuses

The bus station is
1km northwest of the
old town. Turia metro
station is a block away,
and various bus lines
run into the centre
from here, including
79, which is good for
Russafa. A taxi to
anywhere in the centre
will cost €4 to €6.

Getting Around

Public Transport

o Valencia has an
integrated bus, tram and
metro network.

o Most buses (www.
emtvalencia.es) run
until about 10.30pm,
with various night
services continuing until
around 1.30am (3am at
weekends). Pay as you
get on (€1.50), or buy a
Bonobús (€8.50 for 10
journeys), **Bono Trans-**

bordo (€9 for 10 bus or
Zone A metro journeys,
allows changes) or **Bono
Transbordo AB** (€15.50,
includes Zone B also)
at metro stations, most
tobacconists and some
newspaper kiosks.

o Metro (www.metro
valencia.es) lines cross
town and serve the outer
suburbs. The closest
stations to the city cen-
tre are Ángel Guimerá,
Xàtiva, Colón and Pont
de Fusta.

o Part of the metro
network, the tram is a
pleasant way to get to
the beach and port. Pick
it up at Pont de Fusta or
where it intersects with
the metro at Benimaclet.

o One-/two-/three-day
travel cards valid for the
bus, metro and tram
cost €4/6.70/9.70.

Bicycle

o Cycling is a great way
to get around: the river-
bed park gives you easy
access to most of the city
and there's an excellent
network of bike lanes.

o There are loads of bike
hire places, and most
accommodation can
organise you one too.

o The city-bike scheme
is **Valenbisi**

(www.valenbisi.es) – sign up for a week-long contract (€13.30) at machines at the bike racks or online.

o Other options for bike and/or scooter rental include the following:

Berider (☑ 615 033358; http://berider.es; Calle de Calatrava 4; per day/24hr €50/55; ☺10am-1.30pm & 4.30-8pm Mon-Fri, 11am-2pm & 3.30-8.30pm Sat & Sun)

Cooltra (☑ 963 39 47 51; www.cooltra.com; Calle del Mar 54; scooter per day/week €35/140; ☺10am-2.30pm & 4.30-7.30pm)

Do You Bike (☑ 963 15 55 51; www.doyoubike.com; Calle del Mar 14; per day €9-15, per week €35-40; ☺9.30am-2pm & 5-8.15pm)

Solution Bike (☑ 961 10 36 95; www.solution bike.com; Calle Embajador Vich 13; per day €10-15, per week €40; ☺9am-2pm & 5-8pm)

Valencia Bikes (☑ 963 85 17 40; www.valenciabikes.com; Calle Tapinería 14; bicycle hire per hour/4hr/24h €5/10/15; ☺9.30am-2pm & 2.30-8pm Apr-Sep, to 6pm Jan & Feb, to 7pm Mar, Oct & Nov, closed Dec)

Car & Motorcycle

o Street parking is a pain.

o Underground car parks are signposted throughout the centre. The cheapest central one is at the corner of Calles Barón de Cárcer and Hospital.

o Numerous car-rental firms operate from the airport and city centre.

Taxi

o Taxis are plentiful and cheap; think €10 from the centre to the beach, or €8 to the Ciudad de las Artes y las Ciencias.

o There's a minimum daytime charge of €4 and night charge of €6.

o Companies include **Radio-Taxi Valencia** (☑ 963 70 33 33; www.radiotaxivalencia.es) and **Tele Taxi Valencia** (☑ 963 57 13 13; www.teletaxivalencia.com).

o The PideTaxi app is handy for booking a cab.

Essential Information

Accessible Travel

A majority of sights, some hotels and most public institutions have wheelchair access. Most buses have descending ramps and most metro stations have escalators.

Business Hours

Typical opening hours:

Banks 8.30am–2pm Monday to Friday; some open afternoons and/or Saturday mornings.

Restaurants 1pm–3.30pm and 8pm–10.30pm.

Shops 10am–2pm and 5pm–8pm Monday to Friday, 10am–2pm Saturday.

Bars 4pm–1.30am, to 3.30am Friday and Saturday nights.

Clubs 11pm–6am Thursday to Saturday.

Discount Cards

The **Valencia Tourist Card** (www.visitvalencia.com/valencia-tourist-card; 24/48/72hr €15/20/25) has several options but the main ones give free public transport and free or discounted entry to attractions. The card can be bought at any tourist office, metro customer service point, many hotels and newsstands and a vending machine at the airport too.

Electricity

Type C
220V/50Hz

Type F
230V/50Hz

Emergency

International dialling code	☎ 00
Spain country code	☎ 34
General emergency number	☎ 112
Police	☎ 091

Money

o ATMs are plentiful and accept foreign cards.

o Credit cards are widely accepted in hotels and restaurants, but not bars.

Tipping

Bars Locals very rarely tip, though you may leave a small coin or two for table service.

Hotels Not customary to tip, though a euro or two for carrying bags is appreciated.

Restaurants Not obligatory; Round up or tip up to 5%; 10% is very generous.

Taxis Not expected but many locals will round up to the next euro.

Public Holidays

The two main periods when Spaniards go on holiday are Semana Santa (the week leading up to Easter Sunday) and during July and August.

The following are public holidays in the province of Valencia.

Año Nuevo (New Year's Day) 1 January

Epifanía (Epiphany) 6 January

San Vicente Mártir (Feast of St Vincent the Martyr) 22 January

San José (Feast of St Joseph) 19 March

Viernes Santo (Good Friday) March/April

Lunes de Pascua (Easter Monday) March/April

San Vicente (Feast of St Vincent) 9 April

Fiesta del Trabajo (Labour Day) 1 May

La Asunción (Feast of the Assumption) 15 August

Día de la Comunitat Valenciana (Valencia Region Day) 9 October

Día de la Hispanidad (National Day) 12 October

Todos los Santos (All Saints Day) 1 November

Día de la Constitución (Constitution Day) 6 December

La Inmaculada Concepción (Feast of the Immaculate Conception) 8 December

Navidad (Christmas) 25 December

Responsible Travel

Tourism is having an increasingly heavy impact on Valencia so it is important you consider ways to reduce your footprint. Some steps include:

o Visiting off-season and midweek.

o Spending time and money away from the city centre; exploring the outer barrios helps spread the load.

o Staying in hostels or hotels rather than apartment or informal rentals, as these drive up prices for locals.

o Buying from traditional stores rather than chains.

o Extending your trip by visiting the interior of Valencia province, where there are fascinating towns and villages that merit exploration.

o Respecting local culture and customs and making an effort to speak in the local language(s), even if it's only a few words.

Safe Travel

o Valencia is a very safe city and you are unlikely to have any problems.

o There's a small amount of pickpocketing at major fiestas.

o Theft of unattended belongings at the beach sometimes occurs.

o Don't leave your bike unlocked.

o **COVID-19:** Information on travel restrictions and local regulations can be found at www.visitvalencia.com/en/new-normal-arrives-valencia.

Telephone Services

o Mobile (cell) phone numbers usually start with 6, landlines normally with 9.

o Local SIM cards can be used in unlocked phones. Data packages are the best-value way to stay in touch.

o Roaming charges within the EU have been abolished.

o International access code: ☎00.

o Spain country code: ☎34.

o Local area codes are included in the number.

Tourist Information

The city's tourism website is www.visitvalencia.com. Tourist offices are in the city and at the airport.

Ayuntamiento Tourist Office (☎ 963 52 49 08; www.visitvalencia.com)

Joaquín Sorolla Station Tourist Office (☎ 963 80 36 23; www.visitvalencia.com)

Paz Tourist Office (☎ 963 98 64 22; www.visitvalencia.com)

Love Valencia (www.lovevalencia.com)

Visas

o From 2023, non-EU nationals who don't require a visa for entry to the Schengen Area will need prior visa-waiver authorisation to enter under the new European Travel Information and Authorisation System (ETIAS). Travellers can apply online; the cost will be €7 for a three-year, multi-entry authorisation. See www.etias.com

Language

Spanish (*español*) – often referred to as *castellano* (Castilian) to distinguish it from other languages spoken in Spain – is one of the languages of Valencia. The other is *valenciano* and, while you'll find an increasing number of locals who speak *valenciano*, you will be able to get by with standard *español*. Travellers who learn a little Spanish will be amply rewarded as Spaniards appreciate the effort, no matter how basic your understanding of the language.

Just read our pronunciation guides as if they were English and you'll be understood. Note that (m/f) indicates masculine and feminine forms.

To enhance your trip with a phrasebook, visit **lonelyplanet.com**. Lonely Planet iPhone phrasebooks are available through the Apple App store.

Basics

Hello.
Hola. — o·la

Goodbye.
Adiós. — a·dyos

How are you?
¿Qué tal? — ke tal

Fine, thanks.
Bien, gracias. — byen gra·thyas

Please.
Por favor. — por fa·vor

Thank you.
Gracias. — gra·thyas

Excuse me.
Perdón. — per·don

Sorry.
Lo siento. — lo syen·to

Yes./No.
Sí./No. — see/no

Do you speak (English)?
¿Habla (inglés)? — a·bla (een·gles)

I (don't) understand.
Yo (no) entiendo. — yo (no) en·tyen·do

Eating & Drinking

I'm a vegetarian. (m/f)
Soy vegetariano/a. — soy ve·khe·ta·rya·no/a

Cheers!
¡Salud! — sa·loo

That was delicious!
¡Estaba buenísimo! — es·ta·ba bwe·nee·see·mo

Please bring the bill.
Por favor nos trae la cuenta. — por fa·vor nos tra·e la kwen·ta

I'd like ...
Quisiera ... — kee·sye·ra ...

a coffee	*un café*	oon ka·fe
a table for two	*una mesa para dos*	oo·na me·sa pa·ra dos
a wine	*un vino*	oon vee·no
two beers	*dos cervezas*	dos ther·ve·thas

Shopping

I'd like to buy ...
Quisiera comprar ... — kee·sye·ra kom·prar ...

May I look at it?
¿Puedo verlo? — pwe·do ver·lo

How much is it?
¿Cuánto cuesta? — kwan·to kwes·ta

That's too/very expensive.
Es muy caro. — es mooy ka·ro

Emergencies

Help!
¡Socorro!   so·ko·ro

Call a doctor!
¡Llame a   lya·me a oon
un médico!   me·dee·ko

Call the police!
¡Llame a   lya·me a
la policía!   la po·lee·thee·a

I'm lost. (m/f)
Estoy perdido/a.   es·toy per·dee·do/a

I'm ill. (m/f)
Estoy enfermo/a.   es·toy en·fer·mo/a

Where are the toilets?
¿Dónde están   don·de es·tan
los baños?   los ba·nyos

Time & Numbers

What time is it?
¿Qué hora es?   ke o·ra es

It's (10) o'clock.
Son (las diez).   son (las dyeth)

morning	mañana	ma·nya·na
afternoon	tarde	tar·de
evening	noche	no·che
yesterday	ayer	a·yer
today	hoy	oy
tomorrow	mañana	ma·nya·na

1	uno	oo·no
2	dos	dos
3	tres	tres
4	cuatro	kwa·tro
5	cinco	theen·ko
6	seis	seys
7	siete	sye·te
8	ocho	o·cho
9	nueve	nwe·ve
10	diez	dyeth

Transport & Directions

Where's ...?
¿Dónde está ...?   don·de es·ta ...

What's the address?
¿Cuál es la   kwal es la
dirección?   dee·rek·thyon

Can you show me (on the map)?
¿Me lo puede   me lo pwe·de
indicar   een·dee·kar
(en el mapa)?   (en el ma·pa)

I want to go to ...
Quisiera ir a ...   kee·sye·ra eer a ...

What time does it arrive/leave?
¿A qué hora   a ke o·ra
llega/sale?   lye·ga/sa·le

I want to get off here.
Quiero bajarme   kye·ro ba·khar·me
aquí.   a·kee

Behind the Scenes

Send Us Your Feedback

We love to hear from travellers – your comments help make our books better. We read every word, and we guarantee that your feedback goes straight to the authors. Visit **lonelyplanet.com/contact** to submit your updates and suggestions.

Note: We may edit, reproduce and incorporate your comments in Lonely Planet products such as guidebooks, websites and digital products, so let us know if you don't want your comments reproduced or your name acknowledged. For a copy of our privacy policy visit lonelyplanet.com/privacy.

Our Readers

Many thanks to the travellers who used the last edition and wrote to us with top tips, advice and anecdotes: Caroline Westoby, Chris Welch, Margaret Smith, Marnix van der Veen, Paul Webb, Silvia Cavenago

Andy's Thanks

I'm grateful to all my friends in Valencia, especially Rosa Martínez Sala, Delfina Soria Bonet, Enrique Lapuente Ojeda, Dolors Roca Ferrerfabrega, Richard Prowse and José Vicente Revilla García.

Acknowledgements

Cover photograph: La Catedral (p50), Reinhard Schmid/4Corners © Back cover photograph: Paella, bodiaphvideo/Shutterstock © Images p30-1, clockwise from top left: Sergio Formoso/Getty Images ©; Moonstone Images/Getty Images ©; Rrrainbow/Shutterstock ©; DigitalPearls/Shutterstock ©

Behind the Scenes

This Book

This 3rd edition of Lonely Planet's *Pocket Valencia* guidebook was researched and written by Andy Symington. The previous edition was also written by Andy. This guidebook was produced by the following:

Senior Product Editors
Angela Tinson, Sandie Kestell

Cartographers
Valentina Kremenchutskaya, Anthony Phelan

Product Editors
Sarah Farrell, Will Allen, James Appleton

Book Designers
Hannah Blackie, Clara Monitto

Assisting Editors
James Bainbridge, Charlotte Orr, Rachel Rawling

Cover Researcher
Gwen Cotter, Naomi Parker

Thanks to Ronan Abayawickrema, Imogen Bannister, Fergal Condon, Karen Henderson, Sonia Kapoor, Darren O'Connell, Genna Patterson

Index

See also separate subindexes for:
- 🍽 **Eating p158**
- 🍷 **Drinking p159**
- ✪ **Entertainment p159**
- 🛍 **Shopping p159**

Our Writer

Andy Symington

Andy has written or worked on more than 100 books and other updates for Lonely Planet (especially in Europe and Latin America) and others, and has published articles on numerous subjects for a variety of newspapers, magazines and websites. He part-owns and operates a rock bar, has written a novel and is currently working on several fiction and non-fiction writing projects. Andy, from Australia, moved to Northern Spain many years ago. When he's not off with a backpack in some far-flung corner of the world, he can probably be found watching the tragically poor local football side or tasting local wines after a long walk in the nearby mountains.

Published by Lonely Planet Global Limited
CRN 554153
3rd edition – Jun 2022
ISBN 978 1 78657 578 4
© Lonely Planet 2022   Photographs © as indicated 2022
10 9 8 7 6 5 4 3 2 1
Printed in Singapore